As newcomers to Rochester we have been delighted by the enthusiasm which has greeted our exploration of the City's colourful story. We hope we will excite the curiosity of visitors like ourselves and even surprise readers whose homes and lives are centered on the Medway. There was so much to discover and we have selected events and people who caught our imagination and who, we feel, represent some of the highlights of almost 2,000 years. Everyone has been generous with time and knowledge and we are grateful. In particular, Bob Ratcliffe, of the City of Rochester Society, has been unfailing in his support and help with facts and photographs.

We are very grateful for the time and encouragement of all those we have met in Rochester. In particular:

Huw Jarvis and the staff of the Department of Tourism and Marketing at Rochester Upon Medway City Council..

Kate Woollacott and the ever cheerful staff at the Rochester Upon Medway Studies Centre, especially Pat Salter who read and checked our text.

Michael Moad and the staff at Guildhall Museum

Barbara Marchant of Travels in Time

Dr J Gibson and The Rochester Bridge Trust

The staff of the Historic Dockyard

The staff of the Royal Engineers Museum

The staff at Fort Amherst

Norman Munn, Castle custodian

Thelma Groves, chair Rochester Dickens Fellowship

Ann Carter and the Cathedral staff

Len Wadhams

Alec Salter of Watts Charity

Ann Everitt Principal of Gad's Hill School

Published by The Word Team
54 Borough High Street, London SE1 1XL

Designed by Re:*visions*
35 St Michaels Place. Brighton BN1 3FU

Produced by Print Placement, Sherston, Wilts.

Our thanks to all those who have helped us with illustrations. We have tried to acknowlege them all, but where we have been unable to trace sources we hope we shall be forgiven

CONTENTS

INTRODUCTION	2
THE RIVER	6
THE BRIDGE	10
THE CATHEDRAL	14
THE CASTLE	22
THE BUILDINGS OF ROCHESTER	26
AROUND AND ABOUT	34
COLOURFUL CHARACTERS OF ROCHESTER	40
ROCHESTER AT WORK	58
ROCHESTER AT PLAY	66
BIBLIOGRAPHY	70
INDEX	71

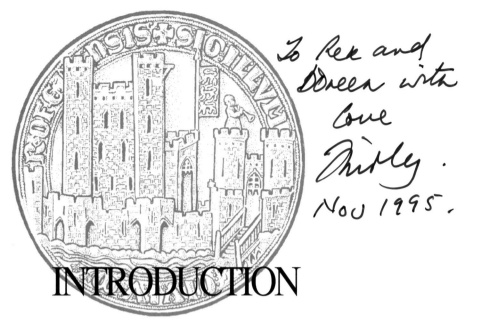

INTRODUCTION

A first sight of the city of Rochester from across the river Medway makes the heart miss a beat. Mysterious through the early morning mist; inviting in the sunshine of summer; dramatic by moonlight. Across the bridge the magnificent castle keep, though passive now, still dominates the river and the city it has guarded for nearly 900 years. By its side the cathedral protects the spiritual well-being of the people.

A historical treasure hunt of the city is best begun in the museum. There are all the clues to set the curious on an exploration of time, beginning with the discovery at nearby Swanscombe of the earliest human remains so far found in Britain. There, face to face, is a skull of Neolithic man, miraculously reconstructed to look almost as handsome as he was 300,000 years ago.

The Romans realised the importance of the river crossing here after the invasion of AD43. They developed the base, which was probably already called Durobrivae, on the river, known then as the Madus. This base became an important fort on the road (later known as Watling Street) linking Chester, London and Europe. It was secured with walls that were 30ft high and 4ft wide and which can, in places, still be seen. Their foundations are 15ft deep.

After the Roman occupation of Britain collapsed, Rochester survived because of its situation on a major highway to Europe. When St Augustine brought Christianity to Kent in AD597, Rochester became his first bishopric after Canterbury.

There followed centuries of tribal invasion by Saxons, Jutes and Angles. Durobrivae probably became Hrofceaster under the Saxons, although there is considerable confusion about the origin of the name Rochester: some sources claim that the town was called after the Jutish leader, Roffen. The river was by this time known as the Medweg.

Saxon cemeteries have been found at Watts Avenue and Roebuck Road, Rochester and on the Great Lines at Chatham. The Chatham burials tend to be Jutish and rather more elaborate, in contrast with plainer, Frankish burials around Rochester.

During the years of Saxon control Hrofceaster became a "burgh", or borough - a fortified place or chartered town. The Domesday book recorded that, in the time of Edward the Confessor, it was a borough valued at 100 shillings. The freemen, holding full municipal rights in these boroughs, were called burgesses and were visited twice a year by the King's representative, his "shire reeve" or sheriff - later, in Norman times, called a bailiff and elected by the burgesses of each borough. He collected taxes.

The Norman Kings legislated by charters. These settled among other things the State religion and provided for its peace and government. Early in the Norman period municipal corporations were formed - according to one French writer these were "a wicked device to procure liberty to slaves"! At first charters for municipalities took the form of exemptions from duty and grants of privilege rather than power. In Rochester some rights and privileges were said to have existed "time whereof the memory of man runneth not to the contrary."

The first grant of definite incorporation was by the charter of King Edward IV in 1461 which was given in recognition of Rochester's loyalty to the Crown: from then on the bailiff was to be called the Mayor and the people became the "citizens" of Rochester. The first Mayor was William Mungeam who gave a supper for the freemen and was allowed £10 for expenses.

The illuminated Customal which lies open, under glass, in the museum dates from 1530 and records the charters of the city, important wills and documents relating to charities, by-laws, customs, enrolments of freemen and the rules and orders for regulating courts. An entry of 1607 refers to the right of Mayors "of every whale to have the head, of every sharkfish to have the heart, of every swordfish to have the head". It has also been embossed with

Guildhall Museum

Houses Gossiping

Rochester upon Medway City Council

the arms of successive Mayors and used in recent years as a visitors' book.

From the reign of Henry VIII, the navy had a major presence on the Medway. Some of Britain's finest sailing ships were built on its broad creeks and safe waters.

Then, in the 18th century came the Royal Engineers who, side by side with the navy, developed military skills and armaments here, which were admired and adopted throughout the world both in war and in peace.

For centuries the streets, the inns, the waterfront were rich in the sounds and smells of water-borne life; convivial soldiers, sailors and fishermen crowded the city which thrived on the trade they brought.

When 4-year-old Charles Dickens came to live by the Medway in 1816, Rochester and Chatham had long been playing a crucial role in the defence of Britain.

Although Dickens' early, idyllic, childhood among the people and places he called "Mudfog and Cloisterham"

was only a flick in the pages of history, Rochester and Chatham together provided him later with the raw materials for his creative genius. They were the "compass points of his imagination".

When eventually he returned in 1856, as a celebrated author to live at Gad's Hill in nearby Higham just beyond Strood, he brought international fame to the towns which had given him so much childhood joy.

Dickens was a journalist, a professional sponge, drawing inspiration from both the dark and light sides of the world around him. The Victorian rural scene he knew so well may have largely vanished today; industry may have besieged the ancient walls and overrun the river banks. But life within those walls is perhaps more tranquil than it was 150 years ago when clattering horse-drawn traffic congested the roads. Traffic is banned now from the High Street, which is so overloaded with architectural delights that almost every building competes for attention. Alleys are overhung by houses gossiping above the heads of passers-by, there are quiet courtyards, secret crypts and ghosts.

Rochester, Gillingham and Chatham, known in their colourful, sea-faring days as "Rob'em, Grab'em and Cheat'em", have, historically, always been linked. But in 1974 the City of Rochester was merged with Chatham and Strood and became the City of Rochester upon Medway. Gillingham currently remains separate.

Today, the motorway roller-coasts

articulated lorries high over the river, on their way to and from Europe and, looking seawards, glass fibre hulls, and jolly pleasure boats have replaced the red-sailed barges and the doble and bawley boats of Rochester's fishing heyday. The last of the old fishing families extract a more modest living from eels.

The elegant buildings of the Dockyard at Chatham have been skilfully adapted to offer an exciting taste of the way things used to be when the yard vibrated to the sounds of up to 13,000 men and women at work. They also house a range of modern, commercially viable, marine-related units.

The Royal Engineers, too, welcome visitors to the splendidly brimming museum which tells their story. The romance of river life is interpreted at the Medway Heritage Centre in a converted Chatham church.

Today's invaders come peacefully, armed only with cameras. From the museums, the exhibitions and the dramatic reconstructions they can learn about the past. They see how the defence of the country depended on the bravery and skill of the Royal Engineers and on the shipbuilding craftsmen and women of the Medway and the sailors who manned the ships they built. There is also the city itself to explore, the river and the surrounding countryside where Dickens rambled. His 20th century readers wear Pickwick weskits, buy Magwitch mugs, and eat in shops named after their favourite characters -

Oliver Twist, Fagin, Mr Pumblechook and the Artful Dodger. He would revel in it all.

Visitors may even meet the Town Crier, in full regalia, who will treat them to a lively "starter-pack" on the colourful story of Rochester. It is a story full of surprises.

The first steam roller was built here, the first guided missile, and the quarter of a mile ropewalk in the Dockyard was the longest brick building in Europe. The rousing outback anthem "Waltzing Matilda" was written in Rochester as a marching tune for the Duke of Marlborough. The wedding cake for the Prince and Princess of Wales took fourteen weeks to make, here, in the kitchens of the Royal Navy School of Cookery. And the rare, wild castle pink, Dianthus caryophyllus, still blooms high on the castle walls.

Rochester High Street around 1880

5

THE RIVER

4,000 years ago, the river threaded its way through swampy marsh and forest to the sea.

By the time the Romans landed in Britain the course of the "Madus" had become more clearly defined. From then on, the river has developed over the centuries not only as a barrier against invaders but also as a thriving commercial freeway. At Rochester Bridge itself, where the river becomes exceedingly rapid "foaming with great noise", much shipping was obliged to stop. Cargoes were transferred into lighters, to be conveyed upwards towards Maidstone or Tonbridge.

For at least four centuries the Mayor has also been titled Admiral of the Medway from Hawkwood to Sheerness. Among the city regalia, the Great Oar represents the power of the Mayor as Admiral, the smaller represents the authority of the Principal Water Bailiff. The Water Bailiffs are freemen, chosen as river police to protect the fishery, whereas the status of Principal Water Bailiff, who is not necessarily a freeman, gives him powers over all shipping on the river.

The charter of Henry VI, in 1446, stated that "Bailiffs and Citizens shall have power to arrest and distrain merchandise shipped or to be shipped in the City, suburbs and precincts within bounds by land and by water

Rochester Castle and Cathedral and River Medway.

to Medeway; also wreck of sea, fish both great and small and other things pertaining to regality as former sovereigns had had.....the Admiral of England his lieutenants and deputies shall not intrude to exercise office within bounds of City by land or sea, but the office of Admiralty there shall belong to the Bailiff and citizens."

But it was the nature of the river itself, with its 18ft tide, deep natural creeks and channels and short reaches, that attracted Henry VIII. From 1547 when he first overwintered his fleet there, the Medway housed a naval base.

Hasted, the 18th century historian, described the lower reaches from Rochester Bridge to Sheerness as "the best, and indeed the only, safe harbour in the kingdom for the larger ships of the royal navy which ride here, when they are put out of commission."

But the Medway is primarily a working river and the traditional sailing craft that once crowded its waters were dobles and bawleyboats and the magnificent barges.

Dobles were heavily constructed of 1in thick oak planking, on sawn ribs. They were about 18ft long with a 6ft beam, providing the necessary weight for them to draw big flue and drag nets. The long, straight spine and double end also made rowing easy.

The Rochester-built bawley boats, each with a 40ft hull, wet well or shrimp boiler and beam trawls, were surprisingly easy to sail. "A pleasure to sail such sweet craft". During the season the men often lived aboard.

There is no sight more stirring, ashore or afloat, than that of the Medway's gentle giants, the red-sailed barges, with their beautiful hand-worked timbers. They carried loads of between 70 to 120 tons: animal fodder for working horses in London, bricks, timber and eventually cement.

The Medway in its commercial heyday

A hulk, a floating tomb

Once aboard, it was the winning huffler's job to lower the sails, so that the boat could be manoeuvred through the eddies whirling around the bridge. They were a tough and wily breed of men - often ex-bargees.

The days of sail were all but over by 1908 when the bawley, Susannah, was launched with a bottle of eau de cologne. She had been fitted with engines. The last wooden barge, Cabby, was launched at Strood in 1928 and is still to be found sailing on the river today. Gradually, the flapping of canvas and creaking of masts gave way to the throb of motor driven boats on the Medway.

Up to 80ft long, they were crewed by one man and a "boy". They could thrash through thumping seas or manoeuvre through creeks and inlets with the greatest of ease. The barge masters were a race of men apart.

The first sailing barges had been built around 1815 at the time of Waterloo. By the mid-nineteenth century 2,433 barges were registered at Rochester alone. Many belonged to the cement manufacturers and brickmakers who had their own yards and ran their own fleets.

In order that these tall-masted boats could pass beneath Rochester

The importance of the barge sailing days has been honoured by the commissioning of a weather vane which sails with the wind from its rooftop position on the Strood bank, outside the Civic Centre.

The age of steam produced a new sight - the paddle steamer - to entertain tourists and holidaymakers. Pleasure boats were accepted, only reluctantly, by the hard working fishermen. Even today yachts and dinghies moored along the river are known as "obstructions" - although they do provide a useful income, which is diverted to help fishermen in need.

> *Fishermen always kept on board some oil of the stingray liver for burns. Tiny gobies were boiled and used as a laxative, the sandpiper (pipefish) was used for whooping cough.*

Bridge and continue up-river, sails and masts had to be lowered by specially skilled men, known as "hufflers". Some were contracted by barge companies while for others there was fierce competition for business. They lurked in the lea of Temple Marsh, watching as the barges approached.

The hulks were in dramatic contrast to the free spirit of the later sailing barges. These sinister, redundant, 18th and 19th century warships had been stripped of masts and rigging and condemned, like the prisoners-of-war entombed within

8

them, to be chained along the banks of the Medway. By 1814, there were 72,000 men in the hulks. In the Brunswick alone, 460 men were sardined on to one deck, 125ft long and 40ft wide. The head room was 4ft 10ins. There was no light, no toilet. There was vermin everywhere. The air was so bad that a candle would not burn. Many of the convicts were used as manual labourers, many were left to rot with nothing at all to do.

The daily ration for these prisoners, dressed only in tattered dirty sailcloth, was 1lb of brown bread and 7oz of beef, 3oz of barley and 1oz onion between four men for midday soup. That was all. Occasionally they were given cod, or herring and potatoes.

Despite this, the soaring spirit of these men was extraordinary. Working secretly, in the near dark, they produced inspired craftwork from nothing - intricate boxes, marquetry, carved bone, woven hair, which they smuggled out to be sold locally.

After 1815 the hulks were used for civilian prisoners who were sent out to extend Chatham docks. The last prison hulk was burnt out on Bastille day 1857.

For centuries the river nurtured dozens of thriving boat-building and repair yards. War ships, cargo ships for timber, barges for coal and cement, passenger carrying paddle steamers and fishing boats had been built there. It was this boat building bonanza at Chatham and Rochester,

combined with the manufacture of iron for munitions in the villages of the Weald, which devastated the forests of Kent, Surrey and Sussex. 2,500 trees were felled for the construction of Nelson's Victory alone. All was transported by water down the Medway.

Until the 19th century the river was a faster, safer means of transport than the road. Today it is much quieter, a haven for houseboats, colourful dinghies, pleasure craft and the occasional converted barge, though it still carries an amount of commercial traffic to the various wharves below Rochester Bridge.

Sailing barge Mary Graham

R.Childs

9

THE BRIDGE

Today the bridge at Rochester carries the only trunk road in Britain which has not been taken over by the Highways Authority.

It is administered, as were most bridges in the past, as a charity paying for its own upkeep. The Rochester Bridge Trust, housed in the former mediaeval Bridge Chapel and the Bridge Chamber on the Esplanade, now consists of 17 Wardens. Formerly these were wealthy landowners, but today the appointments are largely political.

There have been at least six road bridges over the Medway at Rochester. The Romans built one of stone, the piers of which were used by the Saxons in a bridge with wooden spans built in 960. By the 12th century there was a bridge built entirely of timber, to be eventually replaced by a stone bridge in 1392. This lasted until the 19th century when an iron bridge replaced it, the iron arches in turn being replaced with steel ones in 1914.

The foundations of the Roman bridge over the Medway were located in excavations of 1851. This bridge appears to have been constructed on nine stone piers at irregular intervals, and by early mediaeval times carried a flat wooden roadway with no parapets. A steady head was needed to travel across, with the river boiling beneath. Some did not make it.

There are legends galore!

One November evening, it is said, a "befuddled" traveller arrived by horse at the Crown, Rochester. Next morning the landlord, not believing that he could have sucessfully ridden across the dangerous bridge, took him back to look. The traveller was so aghast at what he had done that he fell down dead, with shock.

About the same time, a harper was said to have crossed the bridge and half way over was blown into the river by a gust of wind. He called on the Virgin to save him. She did - and he sang all the time he floated down river watched by an audience on both banks.

In 1339, the Exchequer Accounts for the bridge reveal that it was broken down for twenty four weeks and on several occasions was so dangerous that a ferry was hired to carry travellers across the river.

The bridge finally collapsed under the enormous pressure of melting ice when the river thawed suddenly in 1381.

Building the new, 566ft stone bridge took five years. When it was finished in 1392 it was considered to be superior to any in England (apart from those at London and Westminster). It has been described as "an elegant stone bridge of 11 goodly arches", with a drawbridge at the seventh, to safeguard the city against unwelcome visitors. There were strong battlements and iron rails all along both sides. The bridge was sited, sensibly, slightly upstream and away from the strongest currents.

Kent landowner Sir Robert Knolles had persuaded his friend Sir John de Cobham to join him in helping to finance the building work. It has been suggested that Sir Robert's decision "combined private thanksgiving" for his safe return from fighting in France, "with public beneficence." In 1397 the two men presented a petition to King Richard II, which aimed to safeguard the perpetual maintenance of the new bridge.

The tiny chapel of "Alles solven" (All Souls), which forms the meeting room of the Bridge Wardens, was founded by Sir John de Cobham in 1397 for the spiritual refreshment of travellers and pilgrims. Three priests were appointed to say daily mass and the bridge wardens were responsible for its upkeep

This referred to the already ancient principle, introduced by the Romans, that "certain persons, manors, places, and bounds and landowners" had been bound and charged to make the bridge and be responsible for its upkeep. The petition requested that two wardens should be chosen, in whom maintenance of the bridge was to be vested.

Benefactors (including one "Ricardo Hwytyngton" later to become the real life Dick Whittington, Lord Mayor of London) also gave, or bequeathed, land or gold to the Bridge Trust. It was through rents from this land that funds were amassed to pay for the constantly high cost of repairs.

Seventy five yellowing parchment scrolls tied with ribbon are safeguarded in the Trust's strongroom. These are the accounts for the bridge repairs and maintenance dating from 1398. They were followed in 1576 by velvety leather-bound books which, in

"Mr Pickwick leant over the balustrades of Rochester Bridge, contemplating nature and waiting for breakfast.....Huge knots of seaweed hung upon the jagged and pointed stones trembling in every breath of wind; and the green ivy clung mournfully around the dark and ruined battlements."
(Dickens, Pickwick Papers)

Rochester bridge the new (1914) and the old.

boar, a dragon, a leopard, a talbot and a panther. But the accounts reveal that during 1622 John Vidgeon was paid 4 pence for "setting on the horns of the Booll". The carver himself was also paid 14 shillings for "cutting of a newe Beast & mending of the other that was broken from the drawbridge by overthrowinge of John Clarkes waggon with a load of straw."

During the Civil War, in 1648, the drawbridge played a vital part in the battle of Rochester Bridge, when the Royalists successfully defended the Medway crossing. Five hundred men died in that enterprise. But before leaving the City the Royalists broke up the drawbridge and threw it into the river to prevent the Parliamentarians from pursuing them. Bridge Wardens' accounts for that year record the payment of 1s.6d. to "two menn for saving the planckes of the draw bridge which was throwne into the river by soldiers."

In 1792 the first salaried architect was appointed by the wardens - Daniel Asher Alexander. He was 24 and went on to design the Port of London docks and Maidstone and Dartmoor prisons. His objective was to widen the bridge from 14ft to 26ft, including a footway on both sides. The sixth pier and the arch and drawbridge on either side were removed and the two openings thrown into a single stone arch. The work took 30 years to complete and cost £20,000.

Still there were problems. The narrowness of the arches and the resulting rush of water caused shallows which affected navigation and berthing

painstaking detail, tell the remarkable story of Rochester Bridge.

The Mayor and Corporation were tactfully granted rights of free passage, by ferry, over the river in 1460: "...If and when (which God forbid) it may happen our Bridges there, or any part therof, to want repairing, or be broken, so that a safe passage for our faithful liege subjects beyond the same bridge may not be had...". In 1489, during the reign of Henry VII, the bridge was so rickety again that the Archbishop of Canterbury offered 40 days remission of sins to anyone who would contribute to its repair.

Despite its importance to the city the bridge was always a cause of concern, largely because of mismanagement. Sir William Cecil reported as much to Queen Elizabeth and it was during her reign that an efficient administration was finally established.

Even then the Bridge Wardens were constantly faced with vandalism and accidents. In 1618, during the reign of James I, they had commissioned some decorative carving of the King's royal beasts - a lion, a unicorn, a buck, a greyhound, a bull, a of large ships at Rochester.

There continued to be accidents. In 1816 a party of young revellers set out by boat to celebrate the 21st birthday party of a friend. On the return their boat collided with a plank which had been nailed from pier to pier by workmen repairing the bridge. The boat sank and all passengers including eleven children were drowned.

Only a dog was saved. A last letter from a little girl who died is preserved in the museum.

In 1839 William Cubitt was appointed architect and engineer. His plans were for a fixed cast iron bridge on stone piers in three arches with a fourth opening intended as a swing bridge for the passage of ships with masts. This bridge was finally opened in 1856, amidst fireworks and ceremonial. It had cost £160,000.

Some of the old stone bridge was demolished, the remainder being blown up in 1857 by the Royal Engineers from Chatham using 1,125lb of "villainous saltpetre". The local paper described the event as "a series of grand explosions". The stone was later used to build the Esplanade for public recreation.

In 1865 a urinal for "the accommodation of the public" was thoughtfully constructed, amidst much controversy, at the Rochester end of the bridge.

Concurrent with the planning of the iron road bridge, there were various schemes, one of which came to fruition in the form of a plate girder bridge for the East Kent (later the London, Chatham and Dover) Railway which was opened in 1858. In 1887-1891 the rival South Eastern Railway built a further railway bridge alongside the earlier one which eventually became redundant in 1927 following the formation of the Southern Railway. Meanwhile in 1914 the iron arches of the road bridge had been replaced by steel 'over-road' arches to improve air draught for shipping, thus creating the bridge we know today. Finally, in 1960 the Bridge Wardens bought the redundant bridge and on its piers constructed a second roadway. So now we have two roadways and one railway bridge side by side.

The Traffic Census of April 1890 revealed that, on a Saturday, 17,000 pedestrians and 1,565 vehicles crossed the bridge. On a Tuesday there were 12,776 pedestrians and 1,824 vehicles. That number has risen now to a staggering 55,000 vehicles a day.

According to the Charity Commissioners' ruling of March 1888, the Trust is able to "make contributions to the execution or maintenance of works tending to facilitate the passage over, under or across the Medway."

So today the Rochester Bridge Trust controls the crossing and is also playing a key role in the building of the new tunnel down river between Frindsbury and Chatham. Responsibility for the construction and running of the tunnel has been delegated to the Kent County Council to whom they will pay an annual maintenance charge of £500,000. Thirty years from the anticipated completion in 1996, ownership of the tunnel will revert to the Bridge Trust.

THE CATHEDRAL

Rochester is the second oldest of Britain's bishoprics. Here it was that King Ethelbert, whose wife Bertha was a Christian, built a church and a priory. This was dedicated to St Andrew and is where Justus was ordained Bishop in AD604. The first English born Bishop, Ithamar, was consecrated here in AD644.

Some of the foundations of this long vanished church were discovered in 1889, prior to restoration of the west front of the cathedral. They are marked by brass strips on the nave floor just inside the north west door.

After four centuries of disorder which followed its building, the eventual landing of William the Conqueror in 1066 was in many ways a good thing, bringing with it a period of relative stability. King William decided that a new church was needed in Rochester and he wisely appointed the multi-talented Gundulf as its Bishop.

Gundulf was the King's Chief Engineer, an architect, a mason and a monk who made up for his small stature with prodigious energy. According to the 20th century Rochester writer, Edwin Harris, he is recorded as: "God's soldier under three Kings and by each singled out for honour...to the afflicted and the bedridden and to labouring women he was a most liberal benefactor and endeavoured by his judicious charity to alleviate as far as possible the anguish of disease and the pangs of maternal nature. But he could not endure the faintest praise of his varied excellence."

Gundulf began the new church and established a priory, which he filled with monks of his own Benedictine order. His work was somewhat functional and severe and, though very little of it remains, it can be seen at its best today in the nave arcading and in the western part of the crypt.

Being in such favour with King William, Gundulf was able to manoeuvre all kinds of privileges for his monks and this helped towards financing these operations. He also exchanged useless church land for profitable vineyards; he arranged a share of the toll of Rochester Bridge and gained permission for the monks to sell merchandise in the town. Gundulf shrewdly enclosed the remains of his predecessor, Paulinus, in a shrine of silver, at which many offerings were made. He himself lived in the Bishop's Palace.

The new church had a very narrow transept and no tower. The crypt, which remains, is one of the finest in Britain.

The remains of a free-standing tower of late Norman origin, known today as Gundulf's tower, can be seen to the north side of the cathedral. Its rather stark and sombre, military appearance contrasts curiously with the ecclesiastical atmosphere of the church itself. Today it is used for choir practice.

While all this was taking place, Gundulf began work on the

castle, founded both a nunnery at West Malling and St Bartholomew's Chapel, the hospital for lepers between Rochester and Chatham. In his 'spare time' he built, perhaps his best known achievement, the White Tower at the Tower of London.

Gundulf did not live to see the completion of his cathedral. He died in 1108, and it was his successor Ernulf who finished the work, the cathedral being consecrated on Ascension Day 1130.

Only eight years after its dedication, the new cathedral was badly damaged by fire, which also all but destroyed the city itself.

That year, 1138, marked the beginning of a long period of rebellions and uprisings, in which a great deal of damage was repeatedly done. In particular the sieges of 1215 and 1264 resulted in much pillage, desecration and slaughter.

In 1327, after conflict between the monks and the city,

Rochester Cathedral

Rochester upon Medway City Council

15

R.L.Ratcliffe

16

there were skirmishes with marauding Danes, whose skins were, allegedly, nailed to the cathedral door. In 1343, the central tower was erected, by Bishop Hamo de Hythe, and capped by a wooden spire containing four bells, which he named Dunstan, Ithamar, Paulinus, and Lanfranc.

In 1449 the Bishop's Palace was enlarged by Bishop John Lowe, who is buried in the chapel of St John the Baptist, to the north east of the choir transept. The Dutch scholar, Erasmus, stayed there on a visit to Bishop John Fisher and complained that it lay too close to the river and that its windows let in the unwholesome air!

There appears to have been a King's House, as well as a Bishop's Palace, within the monastic precincts. It was here, in 1540, that Henry VIII had his first, tricky encounter with Anne of Cleves. According to the Windsor Herald of that time, "the King's Grace, with five of his privy chamber being disguised with cloakes of marble, with hoods, that they should not be known, came privily to Rochester and so went up into the chamber, where Lady Anne looked out at a window to see the bull baiting that was the time in the court, and suddenly he embraced her and kissed...but she regarded him little...[so he] put off his cloak, and came in again in a coat of purple velvet...and so talked together lovingly, and after took her by the hand and led her into another chamber, where they solaced Their Graces that night

and until Friday afternoon."

However, it is also recorded that the King was greatly disappointed and "knew not what to say or do". "I am ashamed that men have praised her as they have done and I like her not." It was probably in Rochester that he called her, unkindly, "the Flanders mare".

The best way to picture the palaces the way they were is to climb to the top of the castle and look down on the cathedral and its precincts.

Gundulf's priory did not escape the devastation dealt by Henry VIII during the Reformation. In 1540 he proclaimed that all monasteries must be dissolved and so began the systematic destruction of monastic buildings and the annexation of monastic treasures. The order was less willingly carried out by the Rochester monks than its wording suggests! They were the last to surrender to the Royal Commission. "The prior and convent.....with their unanimous assent and consent, deliberately, and of their own certain knowledge..........especially moving their minds and consciences, and their own free will, gave and granted all that their monastery and the scite thereof, with all their churches, yard, debts and moveable goods, together with all their manors, demesnes, messuages &c to King Henry VIII....."

Immediately, the church was re-dedicated as the Cathedral Church of Christ and the Blessed Virgin Mary of Rochester.

The monuments of Rochester

Opposite: Gundulf, Bishop of Rochester

17

Cathedral, paradoxically, bring to life some of its many celebrated and sometimes eccentric bishops and their flocks .

There was the sickly Bishop Ralph, consecrated in 1108 after the death of Gundulf. He was known as Nugax or the "Trifler", on account of his taste for toys and jests and was later promoted to be Archbishop of Canterbury! There was Walter, in 1147, who hunted until he was over 80 years old and was succeeded by Ernulf, who compiled much of the cathedral's "Textus Roffensis", a collection of ancient records, gifts and privileges. Then there was fundraising Gilbert de Glanville, whose monks sold off the silver shrine of St Paulinus and who were delighted when he died.

Between the north transept and the choir transept, the steps are worn by the feet of many pilgrims on their way to the shrine of St William of Perth. St William was a benevolent baker, who gave away every tenth loaf he baked. He was murdered in Rochester at the start of a pilgrimage to the Holy Land in 1201. Always quick to see a commercial opportunity, the monks set up a rival shrine to that of St Thomas at Canterbury, where, they claimed "he moulded miracles plentifully." The sacrist, sitting in the recess in the north wall, accepted offerings from pilgrims; these were used for repairs and renovations.

Near where St William's shrine once stood in the centre of the north transept, is the magnificent effigy of Bishop Walter de Merton, who founded Merton College, at Oxford University, and was drowned in 1277 during a crossing of the Medway by boat, "there being then no bridge."

Under an arch between John the Baptist's chapel and the presbytery is the most remarkable of all the monuments - the richly decorated effigy of Bishop John de Sheppey, his be-sandalled feet resting on two dogs, each with a red collar adorned with gold bells. The Bishop's eyes and finger ring are examples of the country's earliest use of glass in effigies. Being hidden behind masonry it escaped the destruction that occurred in the early Protestant church. So universal was this destruction that Queen Elizabeth I issued a strong proclamation against "breakinge or defacing of monuments of Antiquitie being set up in churches or other publique places for memory and not for superstition."

Two Bishops whose international renown is, regrettably, not always associated with their cathedral church of Rochester are the Roman Catholic John Fisher, "a man of uncommon learning", and Protestant Nicholas Ridley.

Fisher refused to acknowledge King Henry VIII's self-declared supremacy over the Pope in ecclesiastical matters. So when the Pontiff sent the Bishop his Cardinal's hat, Henry VIII is said to have sworn that he would ensure the Cardinal had no head on which to wear it. Henry executed Fisher in 1535 - when he was 80 years old.

After his death an inventory of the Bishop's possessions was discovered. It included a jar of marmalade - believed in Tudor times to be an aphrodisiac!

Bishop Nicholas Ridley, who became Bishop of London, fell foul of Henry's daughter, the Roman Catholic Mary I, and was burnt at the stake with Archbishop Latimer, in 1554.

Another Bishop who is not buried in the cathedral was Bishop Francis Atterbury (1663-1732). He blotted his copybook by leading a Scottish Jacobite conspiracy against the British throne. "Atterbury's Plot" of 1722 was a failure and the Bishop was sentenced to perpetual banishment in France. Like many Bishops of Rochester at that time he supplemented his inadequate pay by becoming Dean of Westminster as well. When he died, his body was privately interred by his family in Westminster Abbey. On the urn containing his bowels is inscribed: "In hac urna depositi funt cineres Francisci Atterbury, Episcopi Roffensis." But there is no memorial over his grave.

A tale that has grown in the telling is that of Cossuma Albertus. In 1661 this gentleman, claiming to be a Prince of Transylvania, sought refuge from the Germans in the court of Charles II. On the way to London, his carriage became stuck in the mud at Gad's Hill (called by Shakespeare "that woody

> *"'Dear me' said Mr Grewgious, peeping in. 'It's like looking down the throat of old time.'"*
> *(Dickens, The Mystery of Edwin Drood)*

and high old robbing hill"), near Rochester, and whilst he was sleeping he was murdered and robbed by his coachman and footman. The body was discoverd, after a dog retrieved an arm and took it to his master, the local doctor. The prince was buried in style in the cathedral, although the location of his tomb is now uncertain.

The painted, bearded bust of Richard Watts, founder of Watts Charity, leans jauntily from the wall of the south nave transept, while in the south choir transept next to the chapter house doorway is a plaque to Charles Dickens - who wanted to be buried here and whose grave was begun but who was destined, instead, for a place in Poets' Corner, Westminster Abbey.

Largest of the existing tombs is that of Dean Hole - the "Rose King" - who grew 135 varieties in the Deanery garden and whose sleeping marble effigy is strewn with carved flowers.

Rochester is a cathedral in which there is always more to discover. Over two hundred gargoyles, grimacing old men, sober monks and pagan "greenmen" watch over it all and over the visitors who come to admire.

The west front of the cathedral is spectacular with its great Norman door and row of diminishing arches, one inside the other. This is the very entrance through which King Henry

Rochester upon Medway City Council

I walked when he attended the consecration in 1130. Who are the tall, now disfigured, carvings guarding either side of the door? It depends which books you read! Some say Solomon and Sheba, others King Henry I and Queen Matilda.

The superbly preserved remnant of a 13th century fresco of the mediaeval allegory - the Wheel of Fortune - is probably the oldest in England. It was discovered when the pulpit was moved in 1840. In 1867, Sir Gilbert Scott removed the panelling at the back of the old choir stalls to discover that the whole length of the walls had once been painted. He re-produced the golden leopards and fleur de lys on the choir walls.

The elaborate 14th century chapter room doorway, with its sculptural representation of "The Jewish and Christian Church", is said to be one of the finest examples of English Decorated architecture in existence. It leads to the chapter house and library.

Below is Gundulf's crypt, spacious and silent. The rounded arches and later, lighter early English vaulting form seven bays each, originally, with its own altar. Like roots, the columns feel their way into the very foundations of the cathedral where, it is said, lie the remains of St Ithamar and St Paulinus.

The cathedral in Dickens' day had no spire, the mediaeval spire having being taken down in 1825. The present spire dates from 1904 and houses a peal of ten bells.

The spire was to provide an unexpected challenge during the 1920's when, so the story goes, it was scaled by the then Dean's daughter, Monica Storrs. She later went on to be a missionary and was last heard of in Canada.

THE CASTLE

There was probably an ancient British wooden fort protecting the river crossing before the Roman development of Durobrivae. By the late third century a wall with four gates had been built around the town enclosing 23 and a half acres. But it was William the Conqueror who introduced the continental passion for castle building as a means of intimidating and controlling the local population. Castles were symbols of power, owned by the King or by a resident lord, his family, servants and soldiers.

The first Norman construction at Rochester was probably no more than a fortified corral to protect horses. But after the death of King William in 1087 there was much squabbling over the inheritance of his lands on both sides of the Channel. The King's ambitious half brothers, Odo, Bishop of Bayeux, and Robert Duke of Normandy, banded together. Odo seized Rochester because it was an ideal base for raids on London. The brothers were then captured by the new King William II (son of the Conqueror). As a condition of release, Odo promised to restore Rochester, but he reneged on the agreement and shut himself into the town to wait reinforcements.

Meanwhile the King set up a blockade. Then plague broke out. Flies, breeding in the rotting flesh of men and horses, swarmed in the summer heat, filled eyes and nostrils and contaminated food. The men could not eat or drink and comrades took turns to beat the flies away from their companions' mouths with whisks.

Odo surrendered and was sent back to France. The new King also had problems with Bishop Gundulf, who owed him £100. He was concerned that Gundulf had been less than usually strenuous in his loyalty during the troubles with Odo. But the King agreed to wipe the slate clean if Gundulf would design him a stone castle at his own expense. This castle, built of ragstone and rubble, consisted of a single circuit of wall and a gatehouse.

Rochester largely owes today's dramatic, picture post card skyline to the ubiquitous skills of Gundulf the Competent for when he died in 1108 he left plans for the massive internal tower, which was eventually built some time between 1126-1134 during the reign of King Henry I. This keep, with its "frowning walls", is over 100ft high and, dominating the Rochester skyline, remains the tallest in Britain.

In late September 1215, by which time King John was on the throne, his barons, led by William de Albini, seized the castle and tried to block the King's route to London. The castle had no supplies and there was no time to rally provisions.

King John's men attacked, relentlessly. They used slings, catapults, crossbows and five stone throwing machines sited on Boley Hill. On October 26 there was an attempt by 700 barons' men on horseback to lift the siege. This failed. King John ordered his men to begin tunnelling under one of the corner towers, shoring up the excavations with pit props. The besieged men could hear the ominous hammering but could do nothing.

On November 25, the King issued his celebrated order:

"send us with all speed by day and night forty of the fattest pigs of the least good sort for eating to bring fire beneath the tower."

Brushwood and branches were taken into the tunnel with the fat from the 40 pigs. All the timbers caught fire and blazed until they collapsed, the roof gave way and the tower fell down. Even so, there was a strong inner wall behind which the men inside retreated. Food was running out until, eventually, they were compelled to eat their horses. Starvation finally forced them to surrender, on November 30. One crossbowman was hanged and nobles were incarcerated in royal castles throughout the country.

On King John's death (1216) Rochester became a royal castle,

The castle at night

Rochester upon Medway City Council

23

owned by nine year old Henry III. Over the next 15 years the keep was restored and the entire south eastern tower rebuilt to a round, less vulnerable design. By 1248 the building was once more defensible and operational, with improvements having been made to the domestic arrangements.

The remainder of the 13th century saw many uprisings. In 1264 Simon de Montfort attacked the castle. It was then home to Lady Blanche de Warren and her betrothed, Ralph de Capo. Tradition has it that, in a fit of jealous rage, Lady Blanche's rejected suitor, Gilbert de Clare, disguised as de Capo, slipped past the guards and pursued the lady up the corkscrew stairways and along blood-spattered corridors. Eventually her cries for help were heard by de Capo himself. He followed and shot at the intruder but the arrow was deflected from de Clare's breastplate and, instead, pierced Lady Blanche's heart. Her tragic ghost is said to haunt the castle today.

After 1264, the castle lay ruined. Between 1367 and 1380 major works were undertaken to re-fortify it and a new drawbridge was installed. But by the 16th century the castle was obsolete. According to Hasted, at some time during this period an attempt was made to sell the stone and building materials of the great tower. But "the charge of separating and pulling down the stonework was judged to be so heavy an expense that no-one would undertake it on any terms." The crown then gave it to Sir Anthony Weldon whose family held it till 1884. Houses were built in the ditches and the timber floors of the great keep were removed and used in the construction of a brewery; the tower burnt out.

In the 1870's the Rochester Corporation leased the grounds to provide a pleasure park. In 1884 the City Corporation acquired the freehold and in 1965 it was placed in the hands of the state. In 1995 the castle returned to the management of the City Council, the mayor remaining constable of the castle.

THE BUILDINGS OF ROCHESTER

A stroll around the centre of Rochester, starting from Rochester Bridge, is an exercise in visual gymnastics. Up, down, right and left, the city is a feast of architectural treats in the least expected places. There are hidden mediaeval crypts beneath houses in the High Street; a few traces of Watling Street were uncovered at 54 High Street and tucked away behind the cathedral shelters the tea and muffins gentility of Minor Canon Row. But there are other, less well known places with a story to tell, which do not appear in the city's official guided walk.

Newcomers will discover their own favourites from the seemingly endless selection on offer.

THE CROWN *(circa 13th century)now The Norman Conquest, High Street.* "The only place to intertaine Princes coming thither" (Francis Thynne).

The present yellow brick building and adjacent shops in the High Street stand on the site of the city's oldest mediaeval inn, the yard of which is now named Gundulph Square. The Crown became known during the reigns of Edward I and Edward II (1272-1327) because of the philanthropic activities of its master Simond Potyn. Potyn represented the city in seven parliaments. In 1316 he built and endowed a leper hospital "the Spittell of St Katherine of Rochester in the suburbs of Eastgate."

King Philip of Spain and Queen Mary stayed at the Crown: Queen

The Guildhall

Elizabeth spent a night in 1582 on her way to the seaside to meet her suitor, the Duke of Anjou; in 1631 King Charles I was also a guest and in 1732 the cartoonist William Hogarth and a party of friends visited Rochester on a touring holiday. They played hopscotch under the Guildhall colonnade and then spent a rousing evening at the Inn.

Falstaff too enjoyed the hospitality of the Crown in Shakespeare's Henry IV.

THE ROYAL VICTORIA AND BULL
(at least 15th century) High Street
When the Pickwick Club visited The Bull in 1827, Mr Jingle noted "Good house nice beds". Good enough for Queen Victoria too. In 1836, as Princess Victoria, she spent the night at the Bull - hence the change of name. Dickens called the inn "The Blue Boar" in Great Expectations.

THE GUILDHALL *(1687) High Street*
In 1686 "the free gifts of well disposed people" paid for the demolition of a number of old houses in the High Street and the building of the splendid Guildhall in their place. The colonnaded exterior was once the City provisions market.

Admiral Sir Cloudesley Shovel, MP for Rochester, financed the richly ornamental ceiling and decorations in the 47ft long main hall. Approached by a magnificent staircase, the hall is today used for Council meetings and the Admiral's arms are placed alongside those of the Monarch, above the Mayor's chair.

The Crown Inn
Hogarth wrote:

"For our first course a dish there was
Of soles and flounders with crab-sauce,
A stuff'd and roasted calf's-heart beside,
With 'purt'tnance minc'd and liver fry'd;
And for a second course, they put on
Green pease and roasted leg of mutton:
The cook was much commended for't;
Fresh was the beer and sound the port:
So that nem. con. we all agree
(whatever more we have to see)
From table we'll not rise till three."

The cost of this banquet was £1.7s.3d.

The remainder of the building has housed the city museum since 1979. Museum outings are not the dreary affairs they used to be. In Rochester visitors can mint their own money, hear Samuel Pepys' graphic account of the Dutch invasion of the Medway and re-live the sombre reality of life aboard the hulks of the 18th and 19th centuries.

27

The George
crypt

adjacent lane? Whatever its origins, the crypt is almost intact - despite the demolition and reconstruction of successive buildings through 600 years, and despite its use in Victorian times as a skittle alley and a beer cellar. 54ft long and 16 ft 8ins wide, the crypt is divided into four bays and the stonework on the arches and columns is finely ornamented with grapes and foliage and religious gargoyles.

THE CORN EXCHANGE *(1698),*
High Street

THE GEORGE INN *High Street*
("The Crozier" in "The Mystery of Edwin Drood")
The bars of the George Inn are empty; "time" has been called for ever and down the stone steps, leading from the High Street, one of Rochester's hidden treasures lies empty and unseen.

Beneath the pavement an ancient vaulted crypt is all that remains of a once large mediaeval building. Was it a rich man's chapel? Or was it part of the monk's mill which lay at the end of the

The Dickens
Pharmacy

The High Street, said Dickens, is "oddly garnished with a queer old clock that projects over the pavement out of a grave red brick building as if Time carried on business here and hung out a sign."

Originally the premises known now as the Corn Exchange were the Butchers' Market. In the 17th century the site had been occupied by the Guildhall and the main Corn Market was sited at Corn Cross in the middle of the High Street. In the 18th century this building was rebuilt on the common as a centre where children could learn to spin.

In 1706 the beneficent Admiral Sir Cloudesley Shovel donated the money for the present magnificent facade.

It was here in the early 19th century that Charles Larkin, (1775-1833), Rochester auctioneer and lifelong campaigner for civil and religious liberty, set up an alternative Corn Exchange, in protest at the Corn Laws.

On the day of his funeral the shops of Rochester were closed and in 1835

Fine Art Studio, Strood

a 60ft monument was erected in his honour on Telegraph Hill, near Higham.

THE DICKENS PHARMACY *53 High Street*
Number 53 High Street has a hidden claim to fame. When Edwin Harris was writing his "Recollections of Rochester" for the local newspaper, he described it as an old fashioned pharmacy run by a Mr J.B.Frith. This, he said, was the shop patronised by Dickens, who wrote his orders on the desk by the window among a picturesque clutter of bottles and jars. In the cellar were drug mills, belonging to an even earlier time when a chemist made his own tinctures.

Today the premises are a model shop, marked only by an unexplained bust of Dickens above the door.

ABDICATION HOUSE
(now Lloyds Bank), High Street
It was at Abdication House that King James II stayed, under guard, in December 1688 after fleeing from "The Glorious Revolution" led by his son-in-law, William of Orange. Whilst there, he wrote a letter explaining the reasons which had persuaded him to leave Britain but stating that he would remain ready to return at any time if called. He left the house through the back garden and escaped to France by river. At the time the house was owned by Sir Richard Head, Mayor of Rochester in 1664 and 1671 and MP in 1678.

POOR TRAVELLERS' HOUSE *High Street*
Richard Watts (died 1579) was Purveyor to the King's Ships and Collector of Revenues for the Rochester Bridge Trust. In 1563 he was elected

The Poor Travellers House

29

MP for Rochester.

When he died he left part of his large estate to fund a charity to provide, amongst other things, new accommodation to be added to the rear of the already existing almshouses near the Market Cross.

He suggested "six several rooms with chimneys for the comfort placing and abiding of the poor...and also to be made apt and convenient places therein for six good mattresses or flock beds, and other good and sufficient furniture, to harbour or lodge in poor travellers or wayfaring men, being no common rogues or proctors (licensed beggars)...and every of the said poor travellers, at their first coming in to have four pence, and they should warm them at the fire of the residents, within the said house, if need be." The payment of four pence remained unaltered until 1934 - when it was raised to one shilling! Many other improvements followed, such as electric lighting in 1935 and electric radiators in the bedrooms in 1936.

The charity in the High Street has now had a continuous record of care and compassion in Rochester for over 350 years.

In addition to providing overnight accommodation for wayfaring men, pauper children were also housed and taught a trade or occupation. "Reason and consideration procure tranquility", wrote one little girl in her exercise book.

The last "Poor Traveller" to knock at the low door seeking overnight accomodation, signed himself "H.C.Burlton", a stevedore's rigger from Chatham. He signed the register on July 16 1940. Like thousands of wayfarers since the charity was founded, he was given a plain but nourishing meal, taken along the narrow passage and out to one of the simple galleried bedrooms, which remain even today.

Not only have labourers and manual workers enjoyed its hospitality. The well thumbed Register of Travellers has been signed amongst others by an accountant, a cartoonist and a journalist, all apparently down on their luck. One claimed to have been "caddy to the King of the Belgians", another wrote "nothing to grumble at if all was like this."

The beds here may no longer be used, but Watts Charity still cares for about 100 elderly people, who live in various almshouses it has built and runs around the City. There are other organisations and projects which have benefitted from the generosity of Mr Watts, including Sir Joseph Williamson's Mathematical School, and Rochester Girls' Grammar School. In 1880, the Trust took over the building of the splendid new public swimming baths on The Esplanade.

Eastgate House

THE FRENCH HOSPITAL *La Providence, Theobald Square, High Street*

This elegant and spacious Regency square was restored after World War II to provide sheltered accommodation for people of Huguenot descent. From the mid 16th century Protestants escaped from religious persecution in France. The Huguenots, as they came to be called, were skilled in finance, industry and the arts and made a major contribution to Britain's developing society. But there were some who needed care and shelter after the ordeals they had suffered and, for them, a hospital was founded in London in 1718. This continued throughout the 18th and 19th centuries but it was evacuated to Horsham during World War II and in 1960 Theobald Square was purchased and converted.

EASTGATE HOUSE *(1590), High Street*

The sign of the stag which can still be seen outside Eastgate House is a rare reminder of days long ago when houses were not known by numbers. The stag is a pun on the name of Sir Peter Buck for whom the house was built. Sir Peter was Mayor of Rochester and Clerk of the Cheque at Chatham Dockyard.

Towards the end of the 18th century the house became a boarding school for young ladies. It remained so until well into the 19th century.

Dickens renamed it "Westgate House" in Pickwick Papers and "removed" it to Bury St Edmunds. In the mystery of Edwin Drood it was the home of Miss Twinkleton's Academy.

Rochester upon Medway City Council

I n 1897 the City corporation decided to honour Queen Victoria's Diamond Jubilee. They bought Eastgate House for £2,000 and there established a museum for Rochester. Eventually, in 1979 the museum was moved to the Guildhall and Eastgate House became the Dickens Centre.

Visitors pass through a vivid, dream-like series of tableaux, meeting the people and places of Dickens' imagination.

They see the elderly recluse, Miss Havisham in her faded wedding dress, Mr. Jingle, the convict Magwitch, young Pip and Edwin Drood. Were he living here today, doubtless Dickens would find their modern counterparts at the tennis club, in the dole queue, selling The Big Issue for the homeless, running a stall at The Womens' Institute, or maybe crewing pleasure trips up river.

Many of those characters were created in the curious Swiss Chalet, which was a gift to the author from French actor, Charles Fechter, and

Plaque from the French Hospital

31

Satis House

arrived at Higham Station, in 1864, in 58 packing cases! Here Dickens was writing The Mystery of Edwin Drood, when he died in 1870. The chalet was re-erected at Eastgate House in 1961.

RESTORATION HOUSE *(1580-1600), Crow Lane*

Dickens described Restoration House in Great Expectations but called it Satis House, the home of the tragic figure of Miss Havisham. He tells how the elderly broken-hearted eccentric hid from the world behind shuttered windows, still wearing the tattered, yellowing dress in which she had been jilted on her wedding day, forty years before. The story tells how she died, alone, during the fire which swept the house.

Restoration House was owned by Sir Francis Clerke and had achieved fame long before Dickens focussed public attention on its fictional occupant.

King Charles II stayed here in 1660

on the night of the 28 May on his restoration to the throne. It was his first night on English soil in 11 years.

THE KING'S SCHOOL *(occupies several buildings around the cathedral)*

The King's School - also known as Rochester Cathedral Grammar School, has a justifiable claim to be Britain's second oldest school. It is most likely that a school was founded by Justus about the same time as Paulinus and Ithamar required boys to train for a literate priesthood. The school song begins "Sing the school of Saintly Justus."

But the first documentary evidence of a school appears in the 13th and 14th centuries.

At the time of the Reformation it was laid down in the Rochester Cathedral statutes that the Dean and Chapter had a responsibility to establish a Grammar school at which 20 poor boys "destitute of the aid of a friend" and "of good natural parts (as far as may be) and disposed to learn" were to be educated and maintained wholly at the charge of the cathedral. Eligible boys were to be not less than nine and not more than 15 years old and able to read and write and with a knowledge of grammar.

The Dean and Chapter were required to appoint and pay a headmaster and teach not only 20 Grammar School boys free of charge but also "others whosoever may come to our school for the sake of learning grammar." The boys were known as Grammar Boys, King's Scholars or

Foundation Scholars. A notable Old Roffensian was Phineas Pett who, in the 17th century, became one of the country's greatest naval architects, responsible for the design of some of our finest ships.

Today education is provided for boys and girls from pre-preparatory to A-levels. The Choir School merged with King's School in 1937.

SATIS HOUSE *(18th century),*
Bakers Walk

Behind the castle keep stands an elegant 18th century mansion. Originally this was a huge mansion which embraced the present Longley House, The Friars and the Old Hall. Queen Elizabeth I stayed here in 1573, and it is said that the owner, Richard Watts, apologised for the smallness and inconvenience of the house, ill-fitted for the reception of so great a princess. The Queen, who spoke fluent Latin, replied with one word - "Satis" (enough).

Dickens featured the name of Satis House in Great Expectations but with literary licence applied it to Restoration House in Crow Lane. Today the house is used by the King's School.

MINOR CANON ROW

In the time of Henry VIII the dwellings provided for minor church officials were described as an "irregular ruinous pile." Although they were repaired, by 1647 a Parliamentary report described Canon Row as "18 several low rooms and five upper ones, in which divers old and decrepit poor people inhabit that did belong to the Cathedral church." These buildings too were demolished and in 1721 the present modestly elegant row was built for minor canons and the organist.

SENTRY SUPPLIES WAREHOUSE
Victoria Street and East Row

Here, in Dickens' time, was probably the site of the former Woodhams brewery described by young Pip in Great Expectations on his first visit to meet the mad Miss Havisham: "the cold wind seemed to grow colder there than outside the gate; and it made a shrill noise in howling in and out at the open sides of the brewery, like the noise of wind in the rigging of a ship at sea... To be sure it was a deserted place...no pigeons in the dovecote, no horses in the stable, no pigs in the sty, no malt in the storehouse, no smells of grains and beer, in the copper or the vat....In a by-yard there was a wilderness of empty casks, which had a certain sour remembrance of better days lingering about them..."

AROUND AND ABOUT

ST JAMES CHURCH *(13th and 14th century), Cooling*

Here, among the gravestones in the churchyard on the desolate edge of the marsh, is where young Pip, hero of Great Expectations, had his first terrifying encounter with Magwitch the escaped convict from the hulks. Here too, are the thirteen sad, lozenge shaped gravestones, described by Dickens as the tombs of Pip's young brothers and sisters.

The children's tombs, St. James Church, Cooling.

Rochester upon Medway City Council

Sir John de Cobham, co-financier of the mediaeval Rochester Bridge, built a castle at Cooling in 1381 to protect London against invasion up the Thames. The fine gateway and much of the curtain wall to the two bailies can still be seen to the west of the church.

ST BARTHOLOMEWS *(1078), High Street, Chatham*

Bishop Gundulf built a chapel and hospital for lepers and poor people on the site in 1078, making this one of the oldest hospitals in Britain. The chapel remains today. It was restored in 1896.

Income for the hospital and chapel was always meagre; the Benedictine monks relied largely on endowments and when William Lambarde undertook his "Perambulation through Kent" in 1570, he described it as a "poor show of a decayed hospital." So poor and small, in fact, that it escaped dissolution under Henry VIII.

At the start of the 17th century part of the endowment, land adjoining Chatham Dockyard, suddenly became valuable and much sought after by speculators. There was a Chancery action and the Hospital title was upheld. The Deans of Rochester, as patrons of the charity, then pocketed lump sum payments made by tenants when leases were renewed. From these "not inconsiderable" sums the Deans paid the chapel chaplain a stipend, keeping the rest for themselves. In 1836 Charity Commissioners discovered their secret. Dean Stevens, 1822-1835, had received £5,707.7s.10d. but claimed it had been spent on grants to the needy. From then on the Commissioners ruled that funds were to be put to new charitable use and shortly afterwards the St Bartholomew General Hospital was founded. The Victorian red brick building overlooks the river at the boundary between Rochester and Chatham. Absorbed by the National Health Authority in 1948 it is now administered by the Medway Health Authority. It no longer caters for in-patients but it has a continuing role in day care.

11 ORDNANCE TERRACE *Chatham*
The hayfield where the young and delicate Charles Dickens played, opposite his house at No 2 (now number 11) Ordnance Terrace, was dug out for Chatham railway station.

The smell of that place, overlooking the docks, haunted Dickens all his life: "an agreeable scent of pitch, tar, coals and rope yard, a roving population in oilskin hats, a pretty steady influx of drunken bargemen and a great many other maritime advantages." It was in this house that he said he "beat violently against the gates of the world." Here he wrote his first plays with young friends to perform to the family. When Dickens was forced to move with his parents to London in 1821, he left after five happy years "everything that gave my life sunshine."

SIR JOSEPH WILLIAMSON'S MATHEMATICAL SCHOOL
Maidstone Road
Samuel Pepys, who had something to say about most people, originally described Sir Joseph Williamson, MP for Rochester 1689-1701, as a "knowing man and a scholar but it may be he thinks himself to be too much so." Later he called him "a very fine gentleman".

Sir Joseph was President of the Royal Society, one of Charles II's principal Secretaries of State and an academic. When he died, in 1701, he left £5,000 to found a free school for the education of sons of Freemen "towards the Mathematics and all other things which might fit and encourage them for the sea service and arts and callings leading and relating thereto." Despite every effort by his widow to block the bequest, the Mathematical School was founded in 1709.

The original school consisted of one large room, with a house for the headmaster, and stood, somewhat insecurely, in part of the filled up city moat in the High Street.

The first "upper master" was the portly and "worthy" Mr John Colson, who Dr Samuel Johnson once described as a scholar of "remote and unnecessary subjects".

A few students, known as "foreigners", came to the school at their parents' expense. The most illustrious "foreigner" was the actor David Garrick, who stayed with the headmaster and studied for a year in 1737.

For many years financial troubles beset the school and its pupils made little impact outside Rochester. The buildings became dilapidated and in 1816 the Freemen of the City held an urgent meeting to protest at the shameful state of affairs. New rules were drawn up and the 19th century saw a more vigorous programme of educational reform and new building. The old school was demolished about thirty years ago to make way for a car park.

The Mathematical School is now predominantly a boys' grammar school but in 1994 the first girls took their places in the sixth form.

GAD'S HILL PLACE (1790) Higham-by-Rochester

An "old fashioned, plain and comfortable" house, Gad's Hill had the spell of childhood memories for Charles Dickens. As a child he had

Rochester upon Medway City Council

seen it on walks with his father and longed to own it - a dream that was finally realised in 1856.

A Victorian home decorating enthusiast, Dickens delighted in planning alterations and adaptations to the house. He tiled the narrow billiard room walls to protect them from cue damage. He enlarged his living room as a private theatre for entertaining his friends to dramatic readings from his books, and he generously installed a dumb waiter after his maid broke her leg on the steep steps to the basement kitchen.

Here, "Venerables", as his adoring grandchildren called him, wrote Great Expectations, Our Mutual Friend, A Tale of Two Cities and the unfinished Mystery of Edwin Drood.

Charles Dickens' chalet

Opposite: Sir Joseph Williamson's Mathematical School. High Street, Rochester, now demolished

Charles Dickens at Gad's Hill

room for 5 weeks. To the family it seemed AGES."

Ironically, this was not an entirely happy period of his life - his favourite daughter made an unsuitable marriage, his brother died, his mother became senile and Dickens himself was separated from his wife and in the throes of a love affair. He spent a great deal of time, very profitably, giving readings of his books in America.

In the late summer of 1860 he went out to the garden, in the pouring rain, and burned all his correspondence - letters from Thackeray, Tennyson, Carlisle, George Eliot, were destroyed by a damp, reluctant bonfire. At the time Dickens wrote "don't look back".

He worked until lunch, sometimes with a cup of his favourite lime tea beside him made from trees in the garden. From 1864 every morning he strolled across the front lawn and down, through the tunnel he had had built, 6ft beneath the road into Rochester, and over to his chalet in the garden beyond. There he wrote and then, wearing his wideawake hat and down-at-heel-shoes, he strode off around the countryside, invariably for as long as he had sat at his desk.

Many visitors came to Gad's Hill, among them Hans Christian Andersen, who was once found on the lawn sobbing because critics disliked his work and who complained that Dickens was perpetually "jolly". When Andersen left, Dickens placed a card above the bedroom mirror in his room. It said "H.C.A slept in this

This is why, when he eventually died in 1870, having collapsed after dinner, he asked that the house should not become a museum and instructed that all his possessions should be sold.

He would be happy to know that the two classrooms he built for his grandchildren and for the children of his staff are used now by the pupils of Gad's Hill School, which took over his beloved home in 1924.

A horseshoe hangs above the entrance hall, just where Dickens nailed it - upside down "so that the luck pours out over those who enter the house."

The living room, where once he performed to his many famous guests, has become the school common room. It is easy to imagine the characters he created, reappearing as ghostly reflections in the huge wall mirror in front of which he rehearsed before a dramatic reading.

The children eat in the conservatory, which was finished only a week before Dickens died. Here too, he wrote his last cheque - a subscription to the Higham Cricket Club, whose grounds can be seen across the lawn.

In the garden, the caretaker tends two tiny graves. "Dick, the best of birds" was Dickens' canary who each evening took a thimbleful of sherry with his master, and "Mrs Bouncer, the best, most faithful, the most loving of little dogs" are buried there.

In 1992 an American admirer of Dickens, Miss "Posy" Barlow, restored the bell in the cupola on the school roof. This was her "thank you" to the school for help with research during a stay there. The bell, which was an alarm bell in Dickens' day, is now rung ceremonially to announce the arrival of any member of the Dickens family. Great grandson Cedric is a Governor. Great grandson David and great great grandson Christopher are also all very supportive of the school.

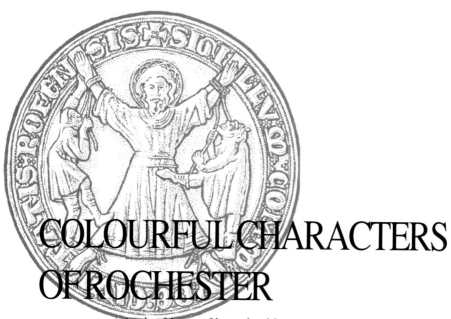

COLOURFUL CHARACTERS OF ROCHESTER

A colourful array of larger than life characters has enriched and refreshed Rochester throughout its history. The famous and notorious are recorded in the museum and in local archives alongside the eccentrics and non-conformists. All are remembered with respect or with affection and humour for their original contribution to the community. Here are just a few of Rochester's better known personalities.

ODO THE ODIOUS *(died 1097)*

Bishop Odo of Bayeux, the Conqueror's half brother, was a greedy, ambitious tyrant, determined to be Pope and also had an eye on the throne of England. He realised that Rochester was an ideal base for pillaging and so it became his headquarters. He is shown many times on the Bayeux Tapestry, probably because he commissioned it!

Odo captured some 200 manors in Kent, stole gold and treasure and buried it in urns in fields and in the river beds, ready for the day he achieved his ambitions. He never did. He died in Palermo, Sicily, while on the First Crusade, unsung and unlamented.

THE PETT FAMILY

Throughout the 17th century, the Pett family was largely responsible for the worldwide pre-eminence of British naval power. They dominated the docks at Chatham, and influenced the development of the royal and merchant navies at Woolwich, Greenwich and Deptford docks.

Phineas Pett (1570-1647), a "verbose and periphrastic" man, first came to Chatham docks in 1600 as keeper of the plankyard and stores. He was largely responsible for almost every ship added to the Royal and merchant navies during the reigns of King James I and King Charles I.

The navy's largest vessel, the Prince Royal, and the extravagantly ornamented, 102-gun, Sovereign of the Seas were, among many, the products of his brilliance.

As a boy, Phineas Pett had been at school in Rochester. He went to Cambridge at the age of sixteen, but after his father's death, in 1589, he was left destitute and ran away to sea. He eventually took a job as a ship's workman at Woolwich docks and began studying mathematics and drawing under Mathew Baker, a friend of the lord admiral, Lord Howard. It was Howard who recognised Pett's talent and eventually sent him to Chatham "with promise of better preferment."

Phineas Pett went on to marry three times and to found a mafia-style dynasty of eight sons and three daughters. He won great favour with King James, in 1603, by building a model ship for the King's son, Henry. As a reward he was appointed captain of the tiny vessel.

When, in 1608, a Commission of Enquiry found that Phineas Pett was guilty of embezzlement of stores the King dismissed the case as "frivolous". Phineas Pett's talents were too important for the navy to lose him to a gaol.

In 1630, after an adventurous career, which included chasing Algerian pirates and hosting King Charles's new Queen, Henrietta Maria, Phineas Pett became the first resident Commissioner at Chatham. There he created a beautiful garden, described later by the diarist John Evelyn, with its "potts, statues, cypresses, resembling some villa about Rome."

When he died, just after the Civil War, in 1647, he was buried at Chatham. Phineas Pett was succeeded by his fifth son, Peter. Peter had become Clerk of Works at Chatham at the age of twenty five and by 1647 had been in partnership with

Bishop Odo blesses the banquet (fourth from left).

Peter Pett

his father for twenty years.

Peter Pett's rather rocky relationship with Samuel Pepys, then Clerk of the Acts at the Navy Board, is regularly recorded with vigour in Pepys' diary. He called him a "weak and silly man".

It is true that, behind the scenes at the docks, all was not well. Peter Pett staffed the dockyard with his relatives. In 1651 two shipwrights wrote to the Navy Commissioners complaining of conditions, saying that people were afraid of retaliation by a family "so knit together that the devil himself could not discover them".

The resident preacher, William Adderley, also intervened and tried to speak to Peter Pett himself. "But he takes part with the offenders and upbraids those who complain as meddlers and smothers up abuses, his kindred being concerned therein." The Commissioners decided it was not in the country's interests to have a generation of brothers, cousins and other relations all packed together in one place of public trust. But there was little they could do. Besides this was a time when corruption was commonplace; and so the family remained in control.

Peter Pett masterminded the return of Charles II in 1660, journeying to Scheveningen in Holland "to get all things ready for the King."

Conditions deteriorated even more during Charles' reign (1660-1685). There was a chronic shortage of money, naval warships were allowed to decay, wages were not paid, thieving was rife. Britain relied on merchant navy traders to sustain her position on the high seas.

There were many charges against the Pett family. It was claimed that they entered higher wages in their books than had been paid - and pocketed the profit. They also rifled the stores - one cousin, Richard Holborn, had two coffins made from stolen timber.

But because their genius as naval architects was unsurpassed anywhere in the world, their often corrupt and illegal activities behind the scenes were largely ignored

In 1664, Peter Pett asked Pepys for 1,000 men to repair ships and by March 1665 one hundred vessels had been refitted. Even so, when the Dutch finally sailed up the Medway in 1667, after many years of battling with the British, Peter Pett was not ready. He had warned the Dockyard personnel of the threat on June 6, but did nothing until Sunday June 9, by which time it was too late and his ships were destroyed.

The Dutch raid brought about his downfall. He was accused of using naval vessels to rescue his own "personal chattels". The possessions in question comprised a superb range of model ships which epitomised the entire art of naval construction. Pett believed "The Dutch would have made more advantage of the models than the ships and that the King had had a greater loss thereby." In hindsight he was seen to be correct.

There was an enquiry, led by Samuel Pepys, who recorded that Mr Pett appeared before the court in garments which were "clean out of fashion". The court was not impressed. His patent as a commissioner was revoked and he was imprisoned in the Tower of London for six months and thereafter disappeared from the history books and died soon after, around 1670. Marvell wrote a poem at the time:
"After this loss, to relish discontent,
Some one must be accused by Parliament:
All our miscarriages on Pett must fall:
His name alone seems fit to answer all."

ADMIRAL SIR CLOUDESLEY SHOVEL
(1650-1707)

The somewhat foppish monument to Admiral Sir Cloudesley Shovel in Westminster Abbey does less than justice to the "rough tough" Admiral. He is portrayed in periwig and lace, reclining on velvet cushions. The words above recall only the ignominious manner of his death and not the distinguished details of his seafaring life.

Cloudesley Shovel was Admiral of the Fleet, with a long record of active service all round the world. Even as a boy he distinguished himself for bravery by swimming from one ship to another under fire during the Dutch War of 1666-1667. He was knighted for gallantry in 1689 and was Rochester's Member of Parliament from 1695-1707. During this time, according to the plaque on the new Guildhall: "this hall was ceiled and beautified at the sole charge of the Hon Sir C.Shovell." In 1706 he also paid for the addition of an ornate frontage to what was then the Butchers' Market, and later became the Corn Exchange.

Pressure of naval work meant that he rarely visited the city but it is recorded that he did dine with the Mayor in September 1701, when the banquet cost £15.2s.0d. (£9.11s.8d. being spent on wine).

But Sir Cloudesly Shovel's gallant naval career was cut short in 1707. Returning from the Mediterannean his ship, the Association, was wrecked off the Scilly Islands, due, it was

But Especially the
Sea faring part of the Nation
To whom he was
A Generous Patron and a worthy Example
His body was Hung on the Shoar
And buried with others in the Sands
But being soon after taken up
Was plac'd under this Monument
Which his Royall Mistress has caused to be Erected
To Commemorate
His Steady Loyalty and Extraordinary Vertue

Splendialy recumbant, the tomb of Admiral Sir Cloudesley Shovel

suggested, to an overdose of homecoming celebration. Nine hundred men were drowned. The Admiral's body was thrown ashore alive and found, says local legend, by a woman who, coveting an emerald, removed his jewelry and "extinguished the flickering life".

Many artefacts were recovered from the wreck of HMS Association during exploration in the 1960's, including a silver plate bearing the arms of Sir Cloudesley which is now displayed in the Guildhall.

BALDWIN CHELTENHAM

On September 27 1712, hidden among the accounts recorded in Rochester Council's massive Meeting Day Book, is a heart warming story of High Street bravado and one man's hour of glory.

"Baldwin Cheltenham one of the ffreemen of the said Citty did on the fifteenth day of this Instant September openly and publicly in the High street of the said Citty not only used several very reproachfull and indecent sayings and expressions to Henry Turner Esqr Mayor of this Citty and caused a drum to be beaten in the said High street against the express order and direction of the said Mayor and when the said Mr Mayor ordered the said drum to forbear beating the said Baldwin Cheltenham opposed him therein and ordered the said drum to beat and said that the said Cheltenham was as good a Man as Mr Mayor But also the said Baldwin Cheltenham did on the same day use very indecent reproachfull and disrespectfull words to Mr Robert Curtis one of the Aldermen of this Citty and called him Blockhead and pittifull Mechanick illiterate fellow which doings and sayings are contrary to his oath and duty of a ffreeman of the said Citty and tend to the disgrace and contempt of the Magistracy and government of the said citty and disturbance and disquiet thereof."

Mr Baldwin Cheltenham was accordingly divested of his privileges as a "ffreeman". But there is a terse afterthought, written in the margin of the Day Book alongside this account. It is signed by Mr Recorder Barrell and comments: "I am of the Opinion that this Order is utterly illegal and is contrary to the law."

On February 28 Baldwin Cheltenham appeared before the City Council and apologised. His disfranchisement was annulled and he lived to beat his drum another day.

THE REVEREND ROBERT WHISTON
(1808-1895)

When the Reverend Robert Whiston was appointed head of the Cathedral Grammar School - known as King's School - in 1842 he brought with him 30 private pupils from his previous school: a necessary precaution since his predecessor was reported to "have flogged away every boy but one" (and that was his own son)!

Six years later Mr Whiston made national news when the local uproar caused by "the Whiston affair" even became the subject of cartoons in Punch magazine. He had fallen foul of the Dean and Chapter by vigorously and publicly championing the cause of the Cathedral scholars and trying to win for them better facilities and higher stipends.

First he asked merely that a stove in the school room be moved to provide greater heat and that matting be put in the cathedral where the boarders sat. Then, more seriously, he accused the Dean and Chapter of defrauding pupils by diverting a portion of the boys' due allowance into their own pockets. Whiston wrote a confrontational pamphlet entitled "Cathedral Trusts - Their Fulfilment." It was priced one shilling and sold well.

On June 29 1849, Mr Whiston was sacked - for the first time. But he stoutly retained possession of the school and playground and taught as though nothing had happened. He was sacked again in October. The Dean and Chapter found a small mediaeval room and, of the sixteen boys on the Cathedral Foundation, six started the new term here whilst ten stayed with Mr Whiston.

When the new "official" head was convicted and fined for punishing a boy with undue severity the Archdeacon transferred his own son to Whiston's rival establishment!

Eventually Mr Whiston won the day and was triumphantly reinstated on January 1 1853.

Boys were to receive an allowance, though not as much as he had requested. He died on August 3 1895 at the age of 87. His funeral service was conducted by Dean Hole.

Punch produced a "New Chaunt for Rochester Choir" which began:

46

"We're surprised Mr Whiston,
you this should insist on
Your scandalous charges 'gainst
dignities high:
Putting forth a vile bead-roll,
which proves each Cathedral
A den of thieves, robbing small
boys on the sly!"

DEAN HOLE *(1819-1904)*

Samuel Reynolds Hole, Dean of
Rochester from 1887, was an affable
champion of fox hunting and Sunday
cycling - the archetypal English
country parson. "We have the nave
of our cathedral at Rochester filled
with cyclists," he once said.

A contributor to Punch magazine,
a poet and, as a young man, "always
falling in love", Dean Hole was an
ardent and knowledgeable rose
grower. He filled the Deanery Garden
with over 135 varieties and all through
his life he wrote about and promoted
his passion. His favourite bloom was
the Gloire de Dijon. In particular, he
was responsible, with others, for the
Grand National Rose show of 1850,
"the sweet smell of roses combatting
the stench invading London from the
Thames". His writer friend, William
Thackeray, called him "the Rose
King".

He himself wrote "he who would
have beautiful roses in his garden must
have beautiful roses in his heart."

The Dean was a great
philanthropist, deeply concerned
about the plight of the Victorian poor,
spending a great deal of time
investigating their living and working

Guildhall Museum

conditions. Even at the age of 75 he
toured America, energetically raising
money for the restoration of the
Cathedral west front.

CHARLES ROACH SMITH *(1807-1890)*

Charles Smith came to live at Temple
Place, Strood from the Isle of Wight.
He was nationally known as the
founder of the British Archaeological
Association and the journal, Collectia
Antiqua. But locally he was respected
as a conservationist. He was especially
keen on the utilisation of barren
railway banks. An enthusiastic
propagator of fruit trees, with a
particular interest in plums, he
unwittingly became the focus of the
traditional rivalry between Rochester
and Strood. He was the originator of

Dean Hole

Opposite:
The Reverend
Robert Whiston

47

a species of damson which he called the Strood Prolific Damson. The name was later changed - to the Rochester Prolific Damson!

EDWIN HARRIS *(1859-1938)*

In his panama hat and white suit, the figure of Edwin Harris was "the very embodiment" of Rochester. There appears to have been no limit to his involvement in local affairs nor his eagerness to write enthusiastically about them.

The son of a local printer, Mr Harris took over his father's business in 1895 and unleashed a torrent of some 60 lively local history booklets and articles on the Rochester public. Although he was an antiquarian and Dickensian authority, historical accuracy was occasionally overwhelmed by a surfeit of romantic enthusiasm when writing about the city. He caught the flavour but not always the facts.

Edwin Harris had an impressive knowledge of Dickens and could recite whole chapters from his books - an admiration that arose, maybe, after Dickens had apparently rescued him, as a child, when his head was stuck in the railings near Rochester Bridge.

He was also, at one time, president of the local United Ancient Order of Druids.

ANNE PRATT *(1806-1893)*

Anne was the daughter of Strood grocer Robert Pratt, who had purchased the freedom of the City of Rochester for £20, and his wife, Sarah, who was of Huguenot descent. Anne was a frail child who took to drawing plants as a "gentle occupation" when she left Mrs Roffey's school in Eastgate House, High Street, Rochester.

The delightfully named garlic treacle mustard, the umbelliforous jagged chickweed and the seaside spurrey sandwort were just three of the wild flowers which she and her elder sister Catherine found as they took long walks around the countryside seeking out specimens for Anne to draw.

Edwin Harris, tour guide

Guildhall Museum

Her first book, "The Field the Garden and the Woodland" was published in 1839 when she was 32. This was followed by "Flowers and their Associations" and "Catechism of Botany and Common Things of the Seashore."

Most of her books were published by the Society for the Propagation of the Gospel or the Religious Tract Society and have a religious slant. The foreword to Volume II of "Wild Flowers" reads: "never was there a time when the direction of our Saviour to 'consider the lilies' more willing followed than now..." She was a typical Victorian lady pursuing the suitable occupations of moral contemplation and flower drawing.

But her delicate drawings were also accompanied by evocative text, crammed full of imaginative asides and unexpected information. "Although the bluebell has no particular use now, in former times it was greatly prized. In days when very stiff ruffs were worn the sticky juice (of the bluebell) was used as starch..." she wrote.

In September 1852 the first volume of "Wild Flowers" was received by Queen Victoria and Anne recorded in the preface to the second edition that she had been "cheered by the Approval of the Highest Lady in the land."

Altogether she wrote 16 books, most of them being in the Rochester upon Medway Studies Centre, Strood.

Very little is known about her personal life. She married very late, in 1866 at the age of 60, and moved from Rochester to East Grinstead in Sussex. She died at the age of 87.

Travellers in Time

Anne Pratt

THE DEFENCE OF THE REALM

The Roman crossing of the Medway in AD43 resulted in one of the most significant battles ever fought on British soil.

The invading army, led by Emperor Claudius, had reached the river on its way north from Dover. Across the water, the general Plautius could see hordes of British warriors massing under Caratacus. Confronted also by the turbulence and unpredictability of the tidal water, he adopted inspired tactics. The army was ordered to begin full scale manoeuvres up-river to divert British attention. Then eight Batavian cohorts, specially trained to swim across rivers in full battle gear, struck out silently and unnoticed to the other bank. There they slashed and killed the British chariot horses. In the confusion that followed two legions successfully crossed the river and established a bridgehead.

The control of that bridgehead has been the reason for so many historic battles in and around Rochester and the river. Over the years, the city has seen many uprisings and rebellions, barons' revolts, confrontations between Roundheads and Cavaliers. Rochester upon Medway has also played an active part in the defence of Britain against foreign intruders.

From 840, for two hundred years, the Danes were a constant threat. In 998 Canute swept up the river "wasting on all sides" and took control of Britain, and so, because of its strategic position on the river, Rochester naturally became a garrison town.

The earliest whispers of a military shipbuilding industry along the Medway belong to the time of King Alfred when Asser (died circa 909) said "at that time did King Alfred command barques and galleys to be built throughout his kingdom that he might engage in a naval battle with those who were newly arriving." It is very likely that some of this fleet was built here, on the Medway.

The Historic Dockyard

It was Henry VIII who, with the encouragement of his surveyors, decided to use the broad creeks and rock-free haven of the river Medway for the winter anchorage of his fleet. This was an ideal resting place for ships waiting to be scraped and refitted. In 1547 Henry hired a large storehouse at 'Jillyngeham' for 13 shillings and four pence a year and so established there the first Naval Base.

Elizabeth I foresaw the urgent need for a truly permanent navy. In 1570 she established the four and a half acre Royal Dockyard on a site named later as Gun Wharf.

In 1583 the first "myghtie chayne of yron" was strung across the river as a defensive measure against Spanish or French warships. It cost £200.

It was here, near the present Sun Pier, that the first warship, the 56 ton Sunne, was launched in 1586.

The most spectacular military confrontation ever faced by the Dockyard took place towards the end of the lengthy Dutch Wars that menaced the British from 1652-1678. Traditionally the Dockyard

> *"The dockyard people of upper rank don't know the dockyard people of lower rank....dockyard people of lower rank don't know small gentry...small gentry don't know trades people - commissioner don't know anybody."*
> *(Dickens, Pickwick Papers)*

produced ships built for action on the High Seas. In 1667 that action came perilously close to home.

At that time, England was reeling from the confusion caused by the Restoration and the extravagances of Charles II, the Plague in 1665, and the Great Fire of 1666 which brought economic chaos. The Royal Navy was in total disarray, the court was corrupt, and

Dockyard figurehead

Rochester upon Medway City Council

The Dutch raid on the Medway

naval officers were squabbling amongst themselves about the best course of action. The fatal decision was taken to cut costs and not refit the battle fleet.

Peter Pett, by then resident Commissioner of the Chatham yard, was said to be a man of "pacific habits and indolent disposition."

The Dutch, under Admiral de Ruyter, watched and waited in their newly refitted ships. On June 11 they sailed to Sheerness and captured it. There was panic. A number of warships were moored across the river to block the path of the oncoming Dutch fleet. The tactic did not work. The invaders sailed on, setting fire to every British ship they passed. The river was ablaze.

On June 14 they broke through the chain that had once again been stretched from shore to shore between Gillingham and Folly Point, where the river is about 500 yards wide. This chain weighed over 14 tons and was supported on four floating stages and manually operated by windlasses. But the weight was so great that it sank nine feet below the surface and was impossible to manoeuvre.

The Dutch boarded the Royal Charles without resistance and this pride of the British navy was ignominiously towed away to Holland. Admiral de Ruyter then sailed up river to watch the final destruction of the Mathias, the Charles V, the Royal James, and the Loyal London. Eight magnificent ships lay blazing in the river that afternoon.

The Dutch lost none. They had sailed into an unknown river and carried out a well-planned, bravely executed raid. The diarist, John Evelyn said it was "a dishonour never to be wiped off."

When the Dockyard was closed

finally in 1984, in the reign of the second Elizabeth, it covered 400 acres of the peninsula, including the marshland known as St Mary's Island. This had been bought in 1855 to provide space for increased facilities needed for the development of iron-hulled ships and the age of steam.

The Royal Dockyard established a glorious record of achievement over a long period of history, during which, in the 17th, 18th and 19th centuries, the British merchant and war ships became the finest in the world. In 1750 over 1,700 men and women were employed there, including caulkers, wheelrights, plumbers, riggers, blockmakers and sawyers. It was a world of its own.

These salty characters may have vanished, but where they worked is now, in part, preserved as the Historic Dockyard - the most complete Georgian dockyard in the world. It contains some 47 scheduled Ancient Monuments. The earliest intact maritime building in Britain is the elegant brick Commissioner's House which is, at present, a banqueting and conference centre.

The spacious waterside walkways form a fine setting for over 80 acres of the Historic Dockyard's stunning naval architecture, much of which has been converted so that visitors can relive those days of the "wooden walls": from Tudor times it was the task of the Navy to keep invading armies from our shores - hence the expressive "wooden walls" for timber hulled warships.

Here, in the gracious white, weatherboarded workshops, in the mould loft and mast houses some of the Royal Navy's finest craft were assembled. Most spectacular of all, the very heart of the docks, are the great covered slips, beached, like upturned boats, along the waterfront.

The "fighting" Temeraire, immortalised by the artist Turner, the Royal James and the Resolution were famous names amongst some 500 ships and submarines launched from this Dockyard. But of them all, the most celebrated is the Victory, launched in 1765, flagship of Admiral Nelson at the Battle of Trafalgar.

Many people had proud memories of this place. Sir Francis Drake learned to sail here when his father was a naval chaplain. William Pitt, the elder, chose Chatham as the title of his Earldom. Diarist Samuel Pepys, "bubbling over with curiosity and excitement", was obsessively knowledgeable about the design and development of ships and was a regular visitor to the docks throughout his brilliant career. A

The Upper Mast House

Rochester upon Medway City Council

53

brass plaque records that Charles Dickens' father, John, was paymaster here.

Visitors to the Dockyard see a site which successfully gives the impression that the vast army of workers has just downed tools and gone for lunch.

During the 19th century, as wood gave way to iron and steel, and sails gave way to steam, much of the labour for building the rapidly expanding Dockyard was provided by convicts from the nearby prison. In competition with Germany, ships became bigger and bigger - they outgrew the Medway. The first major ironclad built in any Royal Navy Dockyard was the Achilles, launched here in 1863.

The last battleship built at Chatham for the Royal Navy was also the largest ever built in the yard. She was the 125m long HMS Africa, launched in 1905.

In 1908 the C17, the first of 57 submarines to be built at Chatham, was the start of a new wave of shipbuilding. During World War I three cruisers and eleven submarines were built and the ships destined for the Zeebrugge raid were refitted. In World War II, 1,360 ships were refitted or repaired here, despite the relentless threat from the air. There were 1,369 air raid alerts between 1940-1945.

The very last Chatham warship was submarine, Okanagan. Built for the Royal Canadian Navy, she was launched in 1966.

In 1984 the Royal Navy severed its links with Chatham Dockyard and four centuries of shipbuilding and repair were ended. The greater part of the site, known as Chatham Maritime, was destined under English Partnerships for redevelopment. The outer basin became a commercial port, operated by the Chatham Dock Company, leaving the Historic Dockyard as an exciting reminder of times past.

Although its natural role, employing nearly two thousand people, is over, marine-linked trades have been encouraged to continue. Ropemaking can be seen in the quarter mile long ropery which was, when built in the 18th century, the longest brick building in Europe. In the old 1720 Sail and Colour Loft, ladies machine sails and flags for the 20th century pleasure sailing fraternity. Ships are also restored and repaired in covered slips and dry docks where they were once built, and in the Ordnance Room skilled craftsmen renovate guns from as early as the 16th century. In a dry dock, the only surviving example of a Victorian naval sloop - the former HMS Gannet - is being carefully restored.

New residential and commercial development also helps to keep the Historic Dockyard alive. The Medway tunnel, when opened, will give almost instant access to the motorway network and bring nearer reality the local authority aim of increased trade and a self-sufficient town-within-a-town.

The Royal Engineers.

Since 1812, when the Duke of Wellington called for the establishment of an engineering school for officers and men, Brompton Barracks in Gillingham has been the headquarters of the Royal School of Military Engineering - the training centre for the Royal Engineers, the Sappers. The Sappers can trace their direct descent from Gundulf, the King's Chief Engineer, appointed by William the Conqueror around 1066.

Visitors to Rochester today have only to look in the Cathedral at the moving list of men of the Royal Engineers who have fought for their country in far flung corners of the world. Honoured leaders: Kitchener, Gordon, Wellington. Famous places: Gallipoli, the Khyber Pass, Khartoum, Sebastopol.

The Barracks has a heart-warming museum which tells the intimate, often surprising and, on occasion, humorous story of a versatile and courageous corps. It is a story reflecting worldwide admiration for the far-ranging technical and scientific skill of the Sappers.

Wherever buildings were needed, from Calcutta Cathedral to Wormwood Scrubs prison in London: wherever roads were constructed, canals dug, railways laid - the Sappers were there. Their name is derived from the old French word for a spade - 'sap', which today means a trench. They were amongst the first military divers, photographers, surveyors; they laid the first telegraph line on active service, built the first guided missile. In times of peace their help is still sought by many foreign governments; in times of war they were - and still are - on the front line, building bridges, harbours, airfields and, above all, clearing minefields. This is a very personal view

Royal Sappers and Miners 1854

Fort Amherst

Kestrels fly free, foxes and badgers play on the high chalk hills and deep recesses which run in a protective semi-circle landward of Chatham Dockyard. The peaceful role of these cliffs today is an illusion. Deep beneath the peace of the nature reserve lies a complex of ice-cold tunnels, vaulted, like a cathedral.

Starting in 1756, when plans were first implemented for the defence of the Dockyard from inland invasion, emaciated prisoners from the hulks and nearby prison were drafted to hack out inch by inch this astonishing, 19 acre network. They worked, in often suffocating conditions, lit only by flame lamps which produced toxic gases. These were removed as far as possible by ventilation shafts such as the dramatic 31 metre "Great Shaft" which some people believe may be of prehistoric origin.

The tunnels were designed to entrap and facilitate the slaughter of any invading armies. There is not much graffiti down there - those who defaced the walls would have been accused of defacing the King's property, for which the punishment was death.

The Fort itself has magnificent views of the docks and river and, from the look-out posts, the watch could see far away across the Medway valley in the opposite direction, towards the sea. The guns within the Fort point south in the direction of Dover - from whence, it was

The development of Fort Amherst

of war. There are Wellington's field sketches used before the Battle of Waterloo, marked with pencilled troop positions and stained with the blood of his Chief of Staff, William de Howe Lancey. The Chinese Court dress given by the Emperor to General Gordon (1833-1885) after the Ton Ping rebellion is displayed alongside the story of the dog named "Snob" who preferred to forage in the officers' trenches where scraps were of superior quality! Even the first guided torpedo - the Brennan - is given a human face. Its inventor, Louis Brennan, who had a factory in the Barracks, was paid £110,000 for all rights by the War Office. He collected the money, in gold bars, from the Bank of England - by horse and cart!

But most moving of all, are the War Heroes' photographs, alongside the medals they won and letters written home during both World Wars.

City of Rochester Society

believed, the enemy would attack.

The tunnels and surrounding walls, batteries and redoubts, in conjunction with a ring of smaller forts, towers and ditches, together form the Lines. They were built and improved between 1756-1820. Napoleon Bonaparte flexed his muscles many times between 1802 and 1815 but the French never came.

During World War I, some 2,000 troops massed here on their way to France. During World War II, Kent County Council's Civil Defence headquarters operated from within the fortifications and plotted the routes of incoming enemy aircraft. The gas masks, the switchboards, the all-clear sirens remain.

After that War the site became disused. Then in 1981 the Fort Amherst and Lines Trust was formed to establish a living military museum. Within the last few years an impressive restoration scheme has rescued the ruin, making it the only surviving Napoleonic fortress in Britain.

The sounds of military orders and gun-fire echo again around the tunnels. In a macabre twist of history, excited children now join in the colourful battle re-enactments laid on for them here at week-ends.

Overlooking the Medway from Fort Amherst

ROCHESTER AT WORK

Although the Dockyard, boat building, agriculture and fishing dominated the Medway around Rochester and Chatham for centuries, there was always also a little industry. There was salt panning, paper making, copperas production (for dyeing and ink manufacture), oil seed crushing, for which wind and steam powered mills were used.

All along the riverside, in the 18th and 19th centuries, small, family-run boat building yards launched warships and trading vessels from the dozens of inlets and creeks.

One of the best known was at Acorn Wharf, from which ships went all over the world. Between 1791 and 1814 the yard was owned by Charles Ross and his wife, Mary. Before the French Wars the couple had built merchant ships for the Hudson Bay Company, but in 1791, with the rebuilding of the French frigate, l'Aimable, they developed an interest in warships. When her husband died, in 1808, Mary took over the business and went on to launch many gunships. Her portrait is in the museum.

On a smaller scale there were dozens of individual shipwrights, working alongside the makers of sails, oars, blocks and pumps.

The men who built barges and fishing boats were craftsmen, often working alone, with hand tools. All that was needed to set up in business was a hard bank sloping down towards the river. Little capital was required. Planks were sawn in a pit

> *"'The principal productions of these towns,' says Mr Pickwick, 'appears to be soldiers, sailors, Jews, chalk, shrimps, officers, and Dockyard men.'"* (Dickens, Pickwick Papers)

in the yard, masts, spars and other timber work was shaped with an adze - every measurment being judged by eye. The earliest named barge builder was R. Horsnail of Strood, in 1803. Barge building, in particular, increased throughout the century to meet the needs of the brick building and cement industries. Very often fishing boats were

included amongst the "boats of all sorts" made by firms such as Tassell of Strood.

Left: Canal Road Wharves

The Oyster and Floating Fishery

The delectable Dover sole which thrives in the rich waters of the

> *"Whereas time out of mind there hath been an oyster fishery in the River Medway."*
> *The Oyster Fisheries Act of 1728*

Medway, smelt with its "ravenous nature and mouth full of formidable teeth", shrimp, salmon and oysters: all have provided a handsome living through the ages, not only for the fishermen but also for the shopkeepers of the city.

Competition between families was fierce. In the 19th century the Wadhams, the Pococks, the Hills and the Letleys were kings of the river.

It is still the Principal Water Bailiff who summons the freemen to

Bridge Reach, Rochester

the Court of Admiralty, as he has done for over 400 years. They meet annually now at the Guildhall. Today's Admiralty Court has more pageantry than power. But even today, a jury is elected to monitor activities and oversee the river, upholding the

The smelt

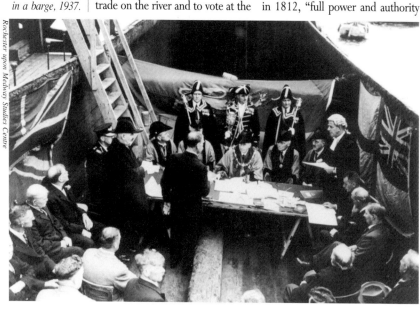

rules and regulations of the industry.

Once a year carrying the great silver oar, symbol of the Mayor's authority, they sail down river to beat the bounds of his jurisdiction from Hawkwood to Sheerness.

Fishing was one of the Trade Guilds of Rochester. As a member of his Guild a fisherman was free to trade on the river and to vote at the

Admiralty Court in a barge, 1937.

Admiralty Court. It usually took seven years to earn the status of freeman although it was also possible to inherit the privilege or, on occasion, to buy it.

Around the age of 14 (it is 18 today), a lad would be enrolled to serve his apprenticeship as a "servant" to an existing freeman - usually his father. He was given pocket money, but no pay. Once he had completed his service he received his "blue paper", with all its responsibilities

In 1995 Mark Edward Pink was accepted as an apprentice by the Admiralty Court. His grandmother was a Letley. In 1992, the Admiral granted Len Wadhams, who was already Chamberlain of the Court, and whose family was fishing the river in 1812, "full power and authority to do execute and perform the duty of the said Office of Water Bailiff ...AND to seize and take into your custody all manner of Wrecks and Sea Flotsam and Jetsum and other Goods and Merchandise which may or can be found floating upon the Waters or Streams..."

In the 19th century heyday of the fishery, when there could be a hundred boats afloat, the river "boiled with fish." Men in smocks worked in co-operatives, often at night, in the eerie, flickering, light of colza oil lamps. The slaughter of fish was huge. Every village had its wharf. Families, with enormous copper cauldrons, worked by the waterside; pedlars carrying produce in baskets toured surrounding villages. But most of the catch went to London and the provinces - even, so they say, to the Royal kitchens.

Although the fishery has shrunk to a mere half a dozen boats today, the old family names are honoured still and sons follow fathers in the family tradition. The freemen of the river still sometimes trawl for fish and shrimps, exercising their exclusive right to use nets in the tideway from Hawkwood to Sheerness.

The biggest threat to the fisherman's living has always been, and still is, the "cable hangers", or poachers, who are not freemen. They sail in illegally and without thought for the future of the industry they "fish the river out".

Many times in the past, fish have been all but wiped out.

The late 18th century historian, Hasted, refers to the scarcity of once plentiful salmon in the river, due to the "largeness and frequency of the men o' war in it." Freak weather too, has taken its toll. Between 1860-64 the winters were so severe that the Medway froze, destroying all stock. The fishery got into debt and the oyster beds had to be leased - often to cable hangers. The freemen were responsible for their share of this debt, and so families were often in fear of losing their homes.

In late 1945, a glut of cod swept upriver and swallowed all the smelts; then whiting gobbled up the shrimps. But fish eventually returned and, according to Len Wadhams, there is now plenty for all, "but men just don't fancy fishing for a living any more."

He claims that the water is not badly polluted. Fishermen are more concerned about the effect on their livelihood of vibrations from traffic through the new tunnel.

Bricks and Cement

The true industrial boom began here, as in other places, in the mid 19th century and with it developed a host of new inter-related, inter-dependent businesses. Not least among these was brewing. By 1840 there were more than 14 breweries in Rochester and Chatham, satisfying the thirst of a fast-growing, hard-working labour force.

The rapid expansion of London brought prosperity, and the banks of

R.L.Ratcliffe

greatest devastation and the greatest prosperity to Rochester. Huge quarries scarred the countryside and everywhere chimneys poured smoke over the Medway valley. Places like Strood and Frindsbury expanded and merged with each other.

Cement was developed in response to the need for building materials which would set under water. It was a cheap material made from low value commodities - chalk and clay. In the early days production was around 50 tons a week. By the turn of the century there were 30 tall brick chimneys crowding the water's edge and 152 chamber kilns. Cement from the Medway was sent to build the Aswan Dam and used in the reconstruction of San Francisco following the 1906 earthquake.

"The Land of Cement" as seen by Donald Maxwell.

'Muddies' collecting river mud for brickmaking

the rural Medway were swallowed by brickyards, cement factories, lime kilns. The bricks for the British Museum and the lime for the new London and Waterloo bridges came from this area.

But it was the growth of industry and the development of cement manufacture which brought the

Life was hazardous for those men involved in quarrying the 100ft chalk cliffs.

Edwin Harris, the local writer, described: "I have seen men, with a life-line fastened round their bodies, securely tied to an iron crowbar driven into the ground at the top and some few yards from the edge of the chalk cliff. There would be several men working at different heights quarrying the chalk, which would sometimes crumble beneath their feet."

The new industries and growing population needed machinery and equipment and so a huge variety of enterprising companies were founded. They made anything, from

Medway Heritage Centre

62

lavatory cisterns to manhole covers. Some became internationally famous.

Aveling and Porter

Thomas Aveling was born on Sept 11 1824. His father died when he was young and his mother moved from Cambridge to Rochester.

Thomas became a farmer at Ruckinge but was always more interested in improving farming machinery and so, in 1850, he set up a small engineeering works in Rochester. By 1856 he had produced a steam plough and been awarded 300 guineas (£315) by Kent farmers.

In 1858 he opened engineering premises at 24 High Street, Rochester. He became an agent for other manufacturers, who built equipment to his design. In 1861, his main works were established at Strood in order to begin construction of his newest ideas on his own account. In 1862, he was joined in partnership by Richard Porter and together they produced an impressive range of traction engines.

During 1862/3 orders poured in from as far afield as Prussia and Australia. The engines were also exported to the United States for work in Central Park.

The traction engine's road speed caused great public concern and so, in 1865, the Locomotives Act was passed, requiring a town speed limit of 2 mph. A man carrying a red flag had to walk in front.

Aveling Porter 9-10 ton convertible road roller 1920

"Steam Sappers", as they were called, were used by the army to pull guns and later served in the Boer War. Aveling's steam ploughs had won him awards at agricultural shows all over Europe.

The road roller, which became his most celebrated achievement, was given its first public trial in Hyde Park in 1866. Road rollers were used extensively during the worldwide road building boom of the later 19th century. Over 10,000 road rollers were built by Aveling and Porter, a number in excess of the total combined output of all other British manufacturers.

Thomas Aveling was a martinet, inspired and irascible. He provided unusually good facilities, including mess stores for hot food to keep his workers from the pubs. Men were also encouraged to participate in running the firm. Aveling was a leading local Liberal, governor of the Mathematical School and patron of Watts Charity.

He caught pneumonia on board

his 28 ton yacht "Sally", and died in 1882 at the age of 58. His son, Thomas Lake Aveling, took over an expanding company that, by 1897 employed 1,000 men.

Success followed success, the very latest machinery and ideas were introduced and the product range increased. During World War I Aveling and Porter raised its own works artillery detachment which was eventually absorbed into the regular forces.

After the war there were major amalgamations and new head offices were opened in London. But by 1930 the company was in trouble. A major fire and the effects of recession were taking their toll. In 1931 Thomas Lake Aveling died and his place was taken by his son, Major Thomas Aveling MC. But there were, by now, only 400 workers remaining and his chairmanship lasted only two weeks. On April 25 1931 a judge issued a compulsory winding up order and the remains of the firm were taken over by Barfords to become Aveling Barford of Grantham. The site at Strood is today occupied by the Civic Centre.

Short Empire flying boat Canopus

Short Bros

In September 1913 the Chatham News reported:

"Messrs Short Bros, world famous manufacturers of aeroplanes ... have entered into negotiations for the acquisition of Tower Field, Rochester."

The Short brothers, Horace, Hugh and Eustace, who were the first British aeronautical engineers, originally had works at Battersea, in London, where they made balloons for the Royal Aeronautical Club. In 1907 they began taking tourists on sightseeing trips over London.

In 1908, the brothers pioneered the manufacture of aeroplanes. An order for six machines from the Wright brothers in America was the first aircraft order in the world.

Their success was spectacular and their impact on life and industry of Rochester greatly welcomed. After the Dockyard they became the city's second largest employers.

Theirs was the first purpose-built aeroplane factory in Europe. They had produced the first craft to take off from a moving ship, and launched the first naval aircraft with wing folding mechanism. The Short sea

Fine Art Studios, Strood

plane was the first to be successfully employed in a naval engagement, and in May 1916 it shadowed German warships before the Battle of Jutland.

In the difficult years between the wars, the brothers cleverly kept the firm alive by adapting their output. They made bodies for buses, cars and even prams.

By the mid-thirties sales were improving and, with the advent of the Empire Mail service, Shorts developed large flying boats to fly to South America, Australia and Canada. In 1938 they formed a partnership with the Belfast shipbuilders Harland and Wolfe. In World War II they built the Stirling heavy bomber and the Sunderland flying boat, the backbone of coastal command and a derivative of the 'Empire' flying boat of 1936. In 1948 the Rochester works were finally closed, production transferred to Northern Ireland and the last sea plane flew over the river Medway.

Short Empire flying boat over Chatham c1938.

ROCHESTER AT PLAY

The narrow streets of Rochester have always been abustle with entertainment - official and unofficial - and buskers, strolling players, Morris men and jugglers are still a traditional sight.

Victorian England saw the start of popular travel for the masses. From the earliest days of holidays with pay, week-end travel and day trips, Rochester and the surrounding countryside had plenty to offer.

Castle and public baths, demolished in the 1960s

VIEW FROM THE BRIDGE OF THE NEW PUBLIC BATHS AT ROCHESTER, ERECTED BY THE MEDWAY BATHING COMPANY 1855.

The Bathing Establishments

In 1850 a "floating vessel of fanciful and novel structure" was designed by Sidney Smirke R.A and moored for river bathing. Octagonal in shape and patriotically striped red white and blue, the raft floated in front of the Esplanade, rather like a Greek temple. The municipal baths, which were built in 1836, were later taken over by Watts Charity and were designed to attract 'liberal patronage'.

"It is a fact", boasted the brochure, "duly verified by chemical analysis, that the water of the Medway at Rochester is more abundantly impregnated with salt than the Thames at any point above the Nore." The admission price to the baths themselves tells a slightly different story! On Monday, with fresh water, it was three pence, on Tuesday admission dropped to two pence, by Wednesday when a dip was less

desirable for the fastidious it cost only one penny. Thursday was clean water day again and so prices returned to three pence.

The Bathing Establishment's successor - the Sports Centre at Strood - is today a far more ambitious affair with its "sumptuous Paradise Health Suite where refreshments can be served while customers take advantage of the two saunas, two jacuzzis, steam room and four sun beds."

"The streets present a lively animated appearance, occasioned chiefly by the conviviality of the military. It is truly delightful to a philanthropic mind to see these gallant men staggering along under the influence of an overflow of animal and ardent spirits: more especially when we remember that following them about and jestering with them affords a cheap and innocent amusement for the boy population."
(Dickens)

will not be permitted to convert the house into a smoking saloon: if females of a certain class will enter, there are slips which they may occupy."

The final performance on the stage of the Theatre Royal took place in 1884. The building, still standing

Inset Sunday school outing, Victorian style

Theatre Royal, now the Conservative Club

The Theatres

"The Theatre", later to become The Theatre Royal, was Rochester's first purpose built theatre and was opened in the late 18th century under the management of Mrs Sarah Baker. She had previously owned several other establishments where "she was always ready to exchange abuse with her customers." She paid £2,500 for The Theatre and in her time such celebrated names as Edmund Kean, Sarah Siddons and Grimaldi were billed to perform on its stage.

In 1860 the theatre was completely renovated and became, according to the advertisements, "clean bright and respectable." "All physical taint" was removed so that "military gentlemen and their imitators

67

Rochester upon Medway City Council

who went on to build a Palace of Varieties with his son Lion. Their star turns included George Robey and Fred Karno; it was Lion who discovered the entertainer "Little Titch."

When the cinema came they competed by installing bioscopes but there was no answer to television and one by one all such theatres closed.

In recent years the story has come full circle and new centres of international music and drama have opened: in a converted wine warehouse, a former church and in the Historic Dockyard itself.

The Pleasure Boats

"All aboard" the Medway Queen, which, for over forty years, took passengers on pleasure trips down the river Medway.

The Medway Queen herself is unique in that she was built for the Medway and spent all her civilian life serving the river. During World War II she was an auxilliary minesweeper and made more trips to Dunkirk than any other vessel. In all she saved some 7,000 people. When she finally retired in 1963, she became a clubhouse at a marina in the Isle of Wight. After an adventurous two decades she is now, once again, on the Medway where she is being lovingly restored as a fully operational passenger steamer by the Medway Queen Preservation Society.

In the meantime, the Kingswear Castle, the last coal-fired paddle steamer in Britain, continues to take

The Sweeps' Festival

on Star Hill, is now the Conservative Club: the portico was demolished in 1972 to make way for road widening.

Down in Chatham, the Music Hall flourished, after modest beginnings in the back room of a pub called the Granby Head (later the Railway Saloon). Father of the Music Hall was impresario Daniel Barnard,

In "Household Words" Dickens recalls his own first theatre outing:

"the sweet, dingy shabby little country theatre, we declared and believed to be much larger than either Drury Lane or Covent Garden.....Dear, narrow, uncomfortable faded cushioned, flea-haunted, single tier of boxes...and the play, when it did begin, stupid, badly acted, badly got up...the refreshments, as administered by kind hands during the intervals of performance, never to be forgotten, oranges, immemorial sponge cakes.."

pleasure trips down river. She was built in 1924, incorporating the 1904 engines of her predecessor, and underwent a ten year restoration by the Paddle Steamer Preservation Society prior to re-entering service in 1984. She now operates from Rochester Pier and Thunderbolt Pier in Chatham's Historic Dockyard.

Rochester has always been a honeypot of a place. Set peacefully by the Medway, in the Garden of England, it has, contrastingly, throbbed with life and energy generated by the river folk, fishermen, boatbuilders, and soldiers and sailors. All this under the watchful protection and calm of the castle and the cathedral.

There are about 150,000 residents in the City of Rochester upon Medway today. Every year their numbers swell by already well over a million visitors.

They come not only to enjoy an exploration of the city but also to take part in the various festivals and revels that take place. In May the black-faced chimney sweeps gather to re-enact a colourful traditional ceremony which dates back to 1735 and possibly much further. They gather and dance, in beribboned tatters, from all over the country to waken Jack in the Green. For Dickens' lovers, Rochester has become a place of pilgrimage and in June local residents, young and not so young, crowd the streets in costume for the Dickens Festival. There is music, dancing, and dramatic performances from the author's best loved books. Visitors may find themselves taking coffee with Miss Havisham or enjoying a pint with Fagin. Those who miss the June festivities have a second chance in December when Rochester is "dressed overall" for a glittering Victorian Christmas. Carol singers, bell ringers, street theatre and chestnuts - all a reminder of the way it used to be.

To meet their needs and make them welcome, there is to be a new Tourist Information Centre in the High Street and a multi-million pound riverside project will eventually provide shops, restaurants and walkways from Rochester to the Historic Dockyard.

The future is bright.

The Medway Queen

R.L.Ratcliffe

69

BIBLIOGRAPHY

A Century of Steam Rolling / Whitehead / pub ran Allen / 1975

A Century of Traction Engines / W.J.Hughes / pub Percival Marshall / 1959

A Dickens Chronology / Norman Page / pub MacMillan / 1988

A Week's Tramp in Dickens Land / William R.Hughes / pub Chapman and Hall / 1891

An assessment of the value and limitations of the admissions to the Freedom of the City of Rochester 1663-1780 / Pat Salter

Archaeologica Cantiana / pub Mitchell and Hughes / 1892

Aveling and Porter Ltd / J.M. Preston / pub North Kent books / 1987

Bricks and Brickies / F.G. Willmott / published privately / 1972

Cement, Mud and Muddies - History of the APCM Barges / F.G.Willmott / pub Meresborough Books / 1977

Charles Dickens' Childhood / Michael Allen / pub MacMillan / 1988

Dickens / Peter Ackroyd / pub Sinclair Stevenson/1990

Dictionary of National Biography / 1893

History of King's School Rochester / edited by L.H.Coulson / 1989

History of Rochester / F.F Smith / pub John Hallewell Publications / reprint 1976

Hogarth's Peregrinations / 1732

Introduction to Dickens / Peter Ackroyd / Sinclair Stevenson / 1991

More Memories. Being Thoughts about England spoken in America. / Dean Hole / pub Edward Arnold / 1894

Report on the demolition of a portion of old Rochester Bridge 1856-7 By the Royal Engineers in the winter of 1856-7 Conducted by Capt. Shaw RE under Col Sendham's direction.

Rochester / Ronald Marsh (City librarian) / pub Rochester City Council / 1974

Rochester Castle Official handbook / R.Allen Brown / pub HMSO / 1969

Rochester Castle / a Handbook for Teachers / Tim Copeland / English Heritage / 1990

Rochester Cathedral / Rev William Benham DD / pub Isbister and Co. ltd / MDCCCC

Rochester in Parliament 1295-1933 compiled by Frederick Francis Smith / pub Simpkin Marshall / 1933

Rochester Upon Medway City Archives:
> Meeting Day Book
> Edwin Harris newspaper cuttings
> The Times cuttings
> The Watts Charity Register of Travelers

Shorts / Donald Hannah / pub Key Publishing / 1983

Shorts / Michael J.H Taylor / pub Janes / 1984

Sketches of Rochester / James Phippen / pub James Phippen / 1862

Steam Rollers in Focus / John Crawley / pub John Crawley 1966

The Bawleymen -Fishermen and Dredgermen of the River Medway / Derek Combe / pub Pennant books / 1979

The Cathedral Church of Rochester / G.H, Palmer BA / ed. Gleeson White and Edward Strange / pub George Bell and sons / 1897

The Charles Dickens Companion / Michael and Mollie Hardwick / pub Murray / 1965

The Childhood and Youth of Charles Dickens / Langton / pub Hutchinson / 1912

The Concise Dictionary of National Biography to 1921 / Oxford

The Dickens Country / F.G.Kitton / pub Black / 1905

The Evolution of the City / pub Medway Borough Council / 1976

The Foords of Rochester / Reminiscences by W. Coles Finch

The History and Topographical Survey of the County of Kent / Edward Hasted Esq FRS and SA M.DCC.XCVIII and folio edition pub MDCCLXXXII

The Language of Flowers / Anne Pratt and Thos Miller / published Simpkin Marshall, Hamilton Kent and Co.

The Memories of Dean Hole. From grave to gay, from lively to severe / Dean Hole / pub Edward Arnold/1894

The River Medway / Howard Biggs / pub Terence Dalton / 1982

The River Medway Valley / William Coles Finch / pub C.W Daniel Cmpy / 1929

The Whiston Matter. The Reverend Robert Whiston versus the Dean and Chapter of Rochester / Ralph Arnold / pub Rupert Hart-Davis / 1961

Traffic and Politics; the construction and management of Rochester Bridge AD 43-1993 edited Nigel Yates and James M. Gibson / pub Boydell Press / 1994

Turn on the Fountain. The Life of Dean Hole / Betty Massingham / pub Gollancz / 1974

Wild Flowers / Anne Pratt / pub SPCK / 1855

INDEX

A

Abdication House 29
Achilles, The 54
Adderley, William 42
Admiral of the Medway 6
Admiralty Court, the 60
Africa, the HMS 54
Aimable, the 58
Albertus, Cossuma 19
Albini, William de 23
Andersen, Hans Christian 38
Asher, Daniel Alexander 12
Aveling and Porter 63–64

B

Baker, Mathew 41
Baker, Sarah 67
barges 5, 7–9, 58
Barlow, Miss Posy 39
Barnard, Daniel 68
Bathing 66–67
bawley boats 5, 7
Bishop
    Atterbury, Frances 19
    Ernulf 15, 18
    Fisher, John 17, 18–19
    Gundulf 14–19, 21, 22–23, 34, 55
    Hythe, Hamo de 17
    Ithamar 14, 17, 21, 32
    Justus 14, 32
    Lanfranc 17
    Lowe, John 17
    Odo 22–23, 24, 40, 41
    Paulinus 15, 17, 18, 21, 32
    Ridley 18, 19
Bishop's Palace 15, 17
Bouncer 39
Brennan, Louis 56
brewing 61
Bridge Chamber 10
Bridge, Rochester 6, 10–13, 15, 34, 48
Buck, Sir Peter 31

C

Capo, Ralph de 24
Castle
    Kingswear 68
    Rochester 2, 6, 15, 17, 22–25, 66
Cathedral, Rochester 6, 14–21, 32, 33, 45, 47, 55
Cecil, Sir William 12
cement 7, 8, 9, 59, 61–62
chapter room, the 21
Charity Commissioners 13, 35
Chatham 3, 4, 5, 9, 13, 15, 30, 31, 34, 40, 41,
    52, 53, 54, 55, 58, 61, 64, 65, 68, 69
    Docks 35, 40, 54, 56
Cheltenham, Baldwin 44–45
chimney sweeps 69
Civic Centre, the 8, 64
Civil War, the 12, 41
Clerke, Sir Frances 32
Cobham, Sir John de 11, 34
Colson, John 37

Corn Exchange

Corn Exchange 28, 43
Cricket Club, Higham 39
Crown, the 10, 26–27
Cubitt, William 13
Customal, the 3

D

Danes, the 17, 50
Dean
    Hole 19, 45, 47
    Stevens 35
Dianthus Carophyllus 5
Dick, the best of birds 39
Dickens, Charles
    4, 5, 19, 21, 27, 28, 29, 31, 32, 33, 34, 35,
    37–39, 48, 54, 69
    Centre 31
    Quote 4, 11, 19, 51, 58, 67, 68
Dobles 7
Domesday book, the 3
Drake, Sir Frances 53
Drood, Edwin 19, 28, 31, 37
Dutch, the
    invasion 27, 52
    War 43, 51

E

Eastgate House 30, 31, 48
English Partnerships 54
Erasmus 17
Esplanade, the 10, 13, 30, 66
Evelyn, John 41, 52

F

Festival
    Dickens 69
    Sweeps 68
Fort Amherst 56
freemen 3, 6, 35, 37, 44, 59, 61

G

Gad's Hill 19
    Place 4, 37–39
Garrick, David 37
Gillingham 4, 52, 55
Gordon, General 56
Great Expectations 27, 32, 33, 34, 37
Great Shaft, the 56
Grimaldi 67
Guildhall, the 4, 27, 28, 31, 43, 44, 60

H

Harris, Edwin 14, 29, 48, 62
Hasted, Edward 7, 25, 61
Head, Sir Richard 29
Hogarth, William 27
Horsnail, R. of Strood 59
hufflers 8
hulks 8–9, 27, 34, 56

I

industry 61–64

K

Karno, Fred 68
Kean, Edmund 67

71

Kent, County Council 13, 57
King
    Alfred 50
    Canute 50
    Charles I 27, 40
    Charles II 19, 32, 42, 51
    Edward I 26
    Edward II 26
    Edward IV 3
    Edward, the Confessor 3
    Ethelbert 14
    Henry VI 6
    Henry VII 12
    Henry VIII 4, 7, 17–18, 33, 35, 51
    John 23
    Philip of Spain 26
    Richard II 11
    William II 22
King's House 17
King's School 32–33
Knolles, Robert 11

L
Lambarde, William 34
Lancey, William de How 56
Larkin, Charles 28
Little Titch 68

M
Marvell, Andrew 43
Mathematical School, the 30, 35, 37, 63
Mathias, the 52
Mayor, the 3, 6, 12, 29, 31, 43, 44
Medway Queen, the 68–69
Medway, the River 2, 3, 4, 5, 69, 10, 11, 12, 17,
    22, 35, 40, 50, 51, 52, 58, 59, 60, 61, 65,
    68, 69
Minor Canon Row 26, 33
Montfort, Simon de 24
Mungeam, William 3

O
Okanagan, the 54
Oyster and Floating Fishery 59

P
Paddle Steamer 8, 68
    Preservation Society 69
Pepys, Samuel 35, 42, 53
Pett
    Peter 42–43, 52
    Phineas 33, 40–42
Pharmacy, the Dickens 29
Pickwick Papers 11, 31, 51, 58
Pink, Mark Edward 60
Pitt, William 53
Plautius 50
Poor Travellers' House 29–30
Potyn, Simond 26
Pratt, Anne 48–49

Q
Queen
    Elizabeth I 12, 18, 33, 51
    Mary 26
    Victoria 27, 49

R
Restoration House 32, 33
Robert, Duke of Normandy 22
Robey, George 68
Rochester Corporation 25

Romans, the 2, 6, 10, 11
Ross, Charles and Mary 58
Royal Charles 52
Royal Engineers, the 1, 4, 5, 13, 55, 70
Royal James 52, 53
Royal School of Military Engineering 55
Royal Victoria and Bull 27

S
Sappers, the 55, 63
Satis House 32, 33
Saxons, the 2, 3, 10
Scott, Sir Gilbert 20
Sentry Supplies 33
shipbuilding 5, 50–54, 58–59
Short Bros 64
Shovel, Admiral Sir Cloudsley 27, 28, 43
Siddons, Sarah 67
Smith, Charles Roach 47
South Eastern Railway 13
St
    Andrew 14
    Augustine 2
    Bartholomew's Chapel 15
    Bartholomew's Hospital 34–35
    James Church, Cooling 34
steam roller 5
Storrs, Monica 21
Strood 4, 8, 47, 48, 49, 59, 62, 63, 64, 67
Sunne, the 51
Swiss Chalet 31

T
Tassell of Strood 59
Temeraire, the 53
The George 28
Theatre Royal 67
Tourist Information Centre 69
Town Crier 5
Trade Guilds 60
Traffic Census 13

U
urinal 13

V
Victory, the 9, 53
Vidgeon, John 12

W
Wadhams 59
    Len 60, 61
Warren, Blanche de 24
Water Bailiff 6, 59, 61
Watling Street 2, 26
Watts
    Charity 19, 30, 63, 66, 71
    Richard 19, 29, 33
Weldon, Sir Anthony 25
Wellington 55
Wheel of Fortune, the 20
Whiston, the Rev Robert 45, 47
Whittington, Dick 11
William of Orange 29
William the Conqueror 14, 22, 55
Williamson, Sir Joseph 35
Woodhams brewery 33
World War I 54, 57, 64
World War II 31, 54, 57, 65, 68
Wright Bros 64

72